The Open University
Educational Studies: A Second Level Course
Personality and Learning Block 8

Block 8
Cultural Influences on Cognition and Attainment

Prepared by Jane Wolfson for the Course Team

The Open University Press

The Personality and Learning Course Team

Richard Argent	Fred Lockwood
Asher Cashdan (Chairman)	John Miller
Beryl Crooks	Edward Milner
Sheila Dale	Caroline Morrow Brown
Rhiannon Davies	John Oates
Ann Floyd	Meg Sheffield
Donald Holms	Sue Vaudin
Arthur James	Roy Webberley
Victor Lee	Joan M. Whitehead
Larry Litt	Jane Wolfson

The Open University Press
Walton Hall Milton Keynes
MK7 6AA
First Published 1976

Designed by the Media Development Group of the Open University.

Printed in Great Britain by
Eyre and Spottiswoode Limited
at Grosvenor Press Portsmouth

ISBN 0 335 06508 2

This text forms part of an Open University course. The complete list of units in the course appears at the end of this text.

For general availability of supporting material referred to in this text, please write to the Director of Marketing, The Open University, PO Box 81, Walton Hall, Milton Keynes, MK7 6AT.

Further information on Open University courses may be obtained from the Admissions Office, The Open University, PO Box 48, Walton Hall, Milton Keynes, MK7 6AB.

1.1

Objectives

When you have completed this block, you should be able to:

1   Specify how cultural differences in language, art, values and socialization practices affect the development of cognitive skills.

2   Discuss the relationship between environmental and cultural variables.

3   Assess the universality of Western concepts of cognitive style, intellectual development and intelligence in the light of cross-cultural research.

4   Outline key features of socio-cultural models of 'disadvantage'.

5   Specify key differences in the 'disadvantaged' child's home and school experience which set him apart from other children.

6   Outline different types of educational programme for the 'disadvantaged' and evaluate some English examples in terms of their rationale and probable effects.

7   Recognize the cultural bias which may occur in all aspects of research methodology, from test construction to evaluation of results.

Block structure diagram

This block has been designed to occupy thirty hours of study, spread over a three-week period. The block structure diagram below shows all the components of the block, where they are to be found and how they relate to each other. The table opposite shows the suggested study times for each component and the estimated level of difficulty for the correspondence text and readings (1 = easy; 2 = moderate; 3 = difficult).

	Correspondence text	Folder	Reader 2	Set Book	Broadcasts
Part 1	**Section 1**				Radio 22 introduces Part 1
	Section 2 Activity 1	Art Sheets 1–4			
	Section 3 Activity 2 Activity 3 Activity 4		Berry (1971)		
	Section 4 Whorf (1940) Activity 5			Searle (1972) Chapters 1, 3, 4, 5	Television 12 links with Set Book and Radio 23; general programme for whole block
	Section 5 Activity 6		Goodnow (1970)		
	Section 6 Activity 7		Bernadoni (1964)		
Part 2	**Section 7** Activity 8 Activity 9		Swift (1968)		
	Section 8 Activity 10 Activity 11		Cazden (1970)		Radio 24 and 25 (linked programmes)
	Section 9 Activity 12 Activity 13				
	Section 10 Activity 14 Boxall (1976)				Television 13 and Radio 23
	Section 11		Cole and Bruner (1971)		

Time allocations

Block component	Estimated level of difficulty	Approximate study time	
		Hours	Minutes
Correspondence text	2	7	15
Readings			
Berry (1971)	3	0	50
Whorf (1940)	2	0	20
Goodnow (1970)	2	0	45
Bernadoni (1964)	1	0	20
Swift (1968)	2	0	45
Cazden (1970)	2	0	45
Boxall (1976)	2	0	45
Cole and Bruner (1971)	2	0	45
Searle (1972) (Set Book)	2	2	00
Folder Material			
Art Sheets 1–4		0	30
Activities			
1 Illusion drawings		0	05
2 Temne and Mende field-independence		0	20
3 Nigerian and American sense modalities		0	20
4 Factors in spatial perceptual development		0	25
5 Codability		0	10
6 Failure to attain the concrete operational stage		0	20
7 Test-taking factors		0	10
8 Social class and achievement		0	15
9 Value judgements		0	10
10 Material conditions of the home		0	05
11 'Examination English'		0	10
12 Educational Grouping		0	10
13 Classroom language		0	10
14 Language Projects		0	10
Broadcasts (including notes and activities)		5	00
Total		23	00

This leaves seven hours of study time to be used for working on assignments, further reading, revision, etc.

Reading

Set Readings

BERRY, J. W. (1971) 'Ecological and cultural factors in spatial perceptual development', *Canadian Journal of Behavioural Science*, 1971, 3, pp. 324–36 (Course Reader,[1] pp. 112–123).

WHORF, B. L. (1940) 'Science and Linguistics', *Technology Review*, 42, pp. 229–231, 247–8 (included in printed text).

GOODNOW, J. J. (1970) 'Cultural variations in cognitive skills', *Cognitive Studies*, 1970, 1, pp. 242–57 (Course Reader, pp. 97–111).

BERNADONI, L. C. (1964) 'A culture fair intelligence test for the Ugh, No and Oo-La-La cultures', *Personnel and Guidance Journal*, 1964, 42, pp. 554–7 (Course Reader, pp. 124–129).

SWIFT, D. F. (1968) 'Social class and educational adaptation', in Butcher, H. J. (ed.) (1968) *Educational Research in Britain*, Vol. 1, London, University of London Press, pp. 282–96 (Course Reader, pp. 130–144).

CAZDEN, C. B. (1970) 'The neglected situation in child language, research and education', in Williams, F. (ed.) (1970), *Language and Poverty*, Chicago, Markham (Course Reader, pp. 145–164).

BOXALL, M. (1976) 'The Nurture Group in the primary school', ILEA (internal report).

COLE, M. and BRUNER, J. S. (1971) 'Cultural differences and inferences about psychological processes', *American Psychologist*, 1971, 26, pp. 867–76 (Course Reader, pp. 165–180).

Set Book

SEARLE, C. (1972) *The Forsaken Lover: White Words and Black People*, Harmondsworth, Penguin (Chapters 1, 3, 4 and 5).

Further Reading

Some of the references at the end of this block are asterisked as suggestions for further reading in particular areas; in no way are they intended as part of your set work on this block.

The booklet, *Social Class and Educational Attainment: A Summary of Selected Research Reports*, is optional reading for Block 8 and it is particularly recommended for those students who feel they lack this background.

Broadcasts

Radio Programme 22, *Why Cross-Cultural Studies?*, introduces Part 1 of this block. Professor Phillip Williams of the Faculty of Educational Studies was involved with this programme. Television Programme 12, *Education in Trinidad*, looks at a culture in transition and the changing beliefs and values which are reflected in the development of a post-colonial education system. The programme raises several issues which are relevant to Part 2 of Block 8, one of which—the nature of West Indian dialect and its usage—is the subject of Radio Programme 23, *Creole Dialect*. Television Programme 13, *Nurture Groups*, provides primary source material on an educational project for 'disadvantaged' infant and junior school children. Radio Programmes 24, *Cultural Bias in Children's Books*, and 25, *Combating Stereotypes*, consider ways in which books may shape children's conceptions of cultural differences, and how the study of books may lead to a more general awareness of bias and prejudice. The Course Team author involved with these programmes was Jane Wolfson.

---

[1]*Wolfson, J. (ed.) (1976)* Personality and Learning 2, *London, Hodder and Stoughton/The Open University Press.*

Contents

Folder material accompanying this block
Art Sheets 1, 2, 3 and 4

Jane Wolfson, Lecturer in Educational Studies, graduated in psychology from Nottingham University. She has previously worked on the Open University course *Urban Education* (E351), and with John Raynor co-edited the two Readers for that course (Raynor, J. and Harden, J. (1973) (eds.), *Cities, Communities and the Young,* and *Equality and City Schools,* both published by Routledge and Kegan Paul/The Open University Press). She has also edited Volume 2 of the E201 Course Reader.

1 Block introduction

1.1 Surinder is eight. Her parents came from India to London when she was five. On her way to school each day she walks past fifteen lamp-posts. She counts them, and at the eighth she pauses and says to herself: 'now I am English'. On her way home from school, at the same place, she says: 'now I am Marathi'. Surinder's world is divided into two: different languages, food, and games; different attitudes to and expectations of her as a child, particularly as a girl, and so on. But the two worlds are not completely distinct; some things are the same, and some of the differences are only superficial. Surinder also remembers the time when they lived in rural India, and she still finds that the endless city streets, the local park, and the cold winters, are strange to her.

1.2 Surinder is imaginary, but in the story of her two worlds lies the theme of this block, which is to consider the implications of growing up in different cultures in terms of personality development and learning. Part 1 contrasts the influences of widely differing cultures; Part 2 is concerned with what happens when, as in Surinder's case, for example, two cultures exist side by side.

1.3 By 'culture' I do not mean simply the art-forms which have earned London, for instance, a reputation as a major cultural centre, but something much broader. Definitions are hazardous, but mine would read like this: 'a word used to describe typical patterns of social, emotional and intellectual behaviours deriving from a shared set of beliefs and values, which are adaptive to the physical environment'. This definition contains two related ideas—that there are typical patterns of behaviour, and that such patterns are adaptive to the environment—and I shall now consider these in turn.

socialization[1]

1.4 To say that there are different typical patterns of behaviour—in socialization practices, artistic representation, etc—is not to deny overlap between cultural groups, or individual differences of experience within any one cultural group. It is not meant to imply that such patterns necessarily remain the same over long periods of time, nor are they completely consistent across all members of a society (hence the notion of *sub-cultures*, cultures within a culture). For example, let us look at some different ways in which concern at the time of a death has been expressed in our own culture, as well as in other cultures.

sub-cultures

---

[1]*Words repeated in the margin are those which are included in the Glossary (p. 113).*

The Diseases and Casualties this Week.

Abortive	2	Grief	2
Aged	24	Griping in the Guts	13
Bedridden	1	Jaundies	6
Bruised	1	Imposthume	6
Cancer	1	Infants	3
Canker	1	Killed by a fall from a Scaffold at St. Martin in the Fields	1
Childbed	12	Lethargy	1
Chrisomes	6	Livergrown	1
Collick	2	Overlaid	1
Consumption	59	Palsie	1
Convulsion	25	Plague	1421
Dropsie	17	Quinsie	1
Drowned in a Tub of VVash in a Brewhouse at St. Giles in the Fields	1	Rickets	8
		Rising of the Lights	3
		Rupture	1
Feaver	82	Scowring	1
French-pox	1	Spotted Feaver	28
Frighted	1	Stilborn	3
		Stopping of the stomach	3
		Suddenly	1
		Surfeit	17
		Teeth	41
		Tissick	3
		Winde	1
		Wormes	8

Christned { Males — 60, Females — 44, In all — 104 } Buried { Males — 951, Females — 855, In all — 1806 } Plague — 1421

Decreased in the Burials this Week — 1413
Parishes clear of the Plague — 26 Parishes Infected — 104

Responses to death in Britain today typically include controlled grief, a family gathering and the showing of 'respects', with an avoidance of details at the time and reminders afterwards. However, the 'quietness' of funerals (funeral teas or 'private service, no flowers please' announcements in the papers) tends to differ in relation to class-linked variables such as the number of relatives counted as 'family', and the length of time spent in one area.

Before medical advances, infant mortality and early death from disease were much more prevalent. Death was more a 'part of life', and probably less shocking; 'memento mori' (a reminder of death) symbols were commonplace.

Cross-culturally, there are many variations in responses to death. The wearing of white, playing of bands, and the gathering of masses at ordinary funerals in Singapore and the Lebanon are illustrated. Anthropologists report that in the Philippines responses include open weeping, detailed factual questioning about the death, a 'vigil' involving offerings of money to the bereaved and a generally merry social gathering.

1.5   Continuing this example for a moment, cultural differences in the length of time between death and burial clearly depend in part on the climatic conditions of the environment. Nearly all discussions of 'cultural' differences lead back sooner or later to differences of physical environment, as the following extract by David Gutman on personality development in a Mexican tribe, shows (Gutman, 1969, pp. 165–6):

projective materials

ecology

. . . in a Lowland Mayan village of the Yucatan, where I collected projective materials from middle-aged and older village-dwelling corn farmers. I also collected data bearing on the typical personality of this group. I did not begin as a naturalist. Working from psychoanalytic bias and theory, I conscientiously made data out of parent–child interaction, weaning, toilet training, disciplining practices, and the location of the child's hammock relative to the parent's hammock. Whenever I wrote about these people however, I always seemed to start with more banal, but also more truly ecological comments. It seemed important that all women dressed alike, or that pigs could wander freely through the house, or that there was a relative absence of straight lines and sharp boundaries in this environment. All these phenomena seemed to be data that were calibrating toward some regularity distinctive of this village, a regularity that set it off from my own accustomed urban American ecology.

My initial approximating statement gives a sense of some of the things that became data for me:

'In the Yucatan, the eye gets trained to flatness and to lack of variation. The eye is constantly pulled horizontally, along the scraggly but generally unbroken line of the bush, over the regiments of hennequen plants, and along the straight extension of the road ahead. The North American eye gets hungry for opposition of line, color, form—for verticals to oppose the horizontals, for clearings in the dusty uniformity of the bush, for stream or lake to contrast the chalky texture of limestone and soil.

In the village, one finds a world whose major events take place at or below the eye level; save for the church, nothing asserts itself with much distinctness, individuality or angularity either against the sky or against the land. Most buildings are alike and have much the same ground plan within their plots, the same conical straw roof, the same white-washed and rounded contours, and much the same uneven boundary walls of white-washed stone. Within the village, the roads meander to avoid an outcropping of the limestone here, a tree there. They do not cut through the landscape, but rather accent it; and at their margins the paths merge, via gradations of underbrush, into the surrounding bush. The domestic habitat is similarly mingled with the terrain; neither the exterior nor the interior of the typical house is sharply distinguished from the natural surroundings. The two realms, the natural (or "vegetable") and the domestic, are interpenetrated; the house floor is of packed dirt, the roof is of thatch. Piles of corn, fodder, and wood at hearthside represent the world of bush and *milpa*. Chickens, dogs, and even pigs move freely from outdoors to indoors and out again, in their search for scraps.

Thus, there is relative lack of distinction between nature and house, between house and house, and, finally, between person and person. That is, dress is not used by the Yucatan Maya to portray individual themes or differences, nor are faces or bodies very expressive of emotion. The men's costume is simple and practical, and relatively invariant from *campesino* to *campesino*; the women's huipils are clean, simple (save for slight touches of embroidery) and similarly invariant.'

1.6   The theme of this block—what it means to grow up in different cultures—can be rephrased as a question: what personality characteristics and what types of learning are required and valued by different cultures, and what cultural conditions foster, or retard, such development? In the text, the influence of 'cultural variables' such as language, art, socialization, schooling and economy will be considered at various points—in each case as they relate to

cultural variables

environmental conditions. Some reference will be made to health and genetic factors; the latter more properly belong in the camp of racial or ethnic group differences, but there are considerable overlaps between racial and cultural groupings. Races within the world population probably originated partly as the result of geographical isolation, and some differences in their inherited physical characteristics are still apparent (e.g., the Semitic nose). But isolation has also led to cultural differences, and it is a matter of debate how far these, or genetic differences, are responsible for differences in intellectual or personality development.

anthropology   1.7   From the strict anthropological point of view, it is irrelevant to attach values of 'better' or 'worse' to different cultures, because they are all equally valuable in the sense that they represent adaptations to different environments. (Adaptation to contact with other cultures is a rather different matter; some groups have undoubtedly survived this much better than others.) But implicit in many psychological attempts to understand cultural differences in cognition and attainment has been the urge to *evaluate* them—usually against the researcher's own standards, on the assumption that his culture is the best,
ethnocentric   and its intelligence the most superior. Such evaluation is called *ethnocentric*.

                        1.8   Inevitably, the use of ethnocentric standards tends to promote a blinkered view in both psychology and education. It ignores the functional value which existing sub- and cross-cultural differences must have by the very fact that they have survived, and leads to a negative view of such differences. Hence the notions, for example, that the intellectual development of 'primitive' man is like that of a Western child; that because certain children (notably working-class and immigrant) fail in school they must be 'deficient' in lan-
compensatory education   guage or stimulation, and be in need of compensatory education. This is not to deny that some differences may represent deficits, that some behaviour may be maladaptive, but rather to highlight the need to bear in mind the question: 'from whose point of view has the assessment been made, and against what standards?'

cultural bias   1.9   Cultural bias is not simply to be found in the evaluation of cultural differences. Naturally enough, the cross-cultural researcher tends to bring to other cultures, and impose on them, descriptive categories and concepts from his own culture. They may fit, they may need modification, or they may be completely inappropriate; and herein lies the researcher's dilemma—how to focus on behaviour in a way that is both meaningful within each culture under study, and across them all. If, as this block is intended to demonstrate, behaviour cannot be rationally considered as context-free, then it could be argued that, to the extent that cultures and environments vary, the researcher is comparing incomparables. But the force of this argument decreases, the more the researcher shows that:

a   he is aware that his instruments of investigation, his whole approach, derive from his own culture;

b   he is prepared to modify his own concepts as an 'outsider' trying to obtain an overview across cultures, to take into account the views which 'insiders' have of their own cultures.

In this way the researcher can establish grounds for comparisons. Of course, it is likely that some behaviours will remain 'incomparable' in the sense that
functional equivalent   they will have no functional equivalent in other cultures.

Block overview

1.10   Part 1 is based on cross-cultural studies which range quite literally around the world, and which illustrate some of the main themes and problems in such research. Sections 2–4 consider factors in the development of perceptual skills,

cognitive style

the role of socialization in the formation of one particular cognitive style, and the influence of language on thought. Section 5 looks at differences in cognitive development within a Piagetian framework, while Section 6 considers whether some cultural groups are more able, more intelligent than others, and in so doing questions how relevant our concepts of intelligence are to other cultural groups.

1.11   Your first reaction to such studies may be to feel that they are nothing more than esoteric research in exotic surroundings. It is true that they contain few direct implications for education in this country, even including provision for children of immigrant cultures. But such studies expose most clearly the influence of culture on personality and learning, and are vital to a more complete understanding of human cognition and attainment. Consideration of much wider variations than we find within our own, or similar cultures, may lead us to question the usefulness of some of our concepts, to revise others, or to generate new, more universally applicable ones. In particular, such variations may illuminate 'nature–nurture' debates about what is 'given' and what 'acquired' in terms of human characteristics, and hence inform our views of educational modifiability. Important too, is the way such studies help us to stand back and look more critically at our own culture. The introductory radio programme for this block, Radio Programme 22, *Why Cross-cultural Studies?* deals further with these issues, while Television Programme 12, *Education in Trinidad*, looks at a culture in transition, at the changing beliefs and

values

values reflected in the development of a post-colonial education system. This programme also raises several issues which are relevant to Part 2.

1.12   Part 2 of this block is essentially a case-study of sub-cultures in England, drawing on some of the ideas in Part 1. It centres on those groups commonly labelled as culturally/socially/educationally disadvantaged, examining the reasons why they are so called. In particular, language differences are considered: Radio Programme 23, on West Indian dialect, grows out of Television Programme 12 and the Set Reading accompanying it (Searle, 1972). Radio Programme 23 also raises the crucial issue of how schools respond to cultural variations and consequent conflicts of values; this debate is taken up both in the correspondence text and in Television Programme 13, which deals with one form of compensatory education, 'nurture groups'. Meanwhile, Radio Programmes 24 and 25 provide a rather different angle on cultural differences: together they form a double feature on the subject of cultural bias in children's books.

1.13   In connection with Block 8 as a whole, there are two cautionary points which I should like to stress: firstly, that research on cultural influences is still very much at the exploratory stage; and secondly that it deals mainly with group differences which will not necessarily hold true for any one individual.

Part One
Cross-cultural studies

2 Perception

retina

Rorschach Inkblots Test

genetic encoding

2.1   The basic fact of perception is that we see *things*. We do not see the bits of colour of different saturation and brightness that distribute themselves in changing patterns across the retina; we see people, trees, houses, and so on. We seek for form to the extent that we can see things in clouds, or flames, or Rorschach inkblots. In Block 4, Section 3, you read about the mechanisms both in the retina and in the brain which 'translate' retinal images into a perceived world of differentiated, relatively stable things. It is still unclear exactly how genetic encoding and learning contribute to the development of perception, but a considerable degree of learning appears to be involved and certainly the perceptual system is very adaptable.

2.2   The *mechanisms* of perception are generally thought to be the same for all people. However, different culture-related habits of *interpreting* visual experience have frequently been demonstrated. For example, the anthropologist Colin M. Turnbull (1961), describing the very first time his Pygmy guide Kenge left the forest to travel to the plains, writes:

. . . Then he saw the buffalo, still grazing lazily several miles away, far down below. He turned to me and said, 'What insects are those?' At first I hardly understood; then I realized that in the forest the range of vision is so limited that there is no great need to make an automatic allowance for distance when judging size.

In our culture, on the other hand, we are used to allowing for distance when judging size. Although our retinal image of a person seen in the distance is smaller than that of a person seen nearby, we do not believe the former to be a midget and the latter a giant; we infer both to be normal sized human beings ('size constancy').

perceptual inference habits

perspective

2.3   Interpretation is the essence of perception, and the above examples serve to illustrate how cultures may vary in their perceptual inference habits. Cross-cultural research on perception has mostly used pictorial materials rather than real-life situations, and in this section we shall be looking at studies using either illusion drawings or pictures drawn in a Western perspective style. Such research both highlights the complexity of cultural influences on perception and exposes some of the assumptions implicit in the use of visual aids in the learning situation. Pictorial material is often considered a lingua franca, unambiguously interpretable by all. But if you have ever been baffled by a diagram or a poster you will know that this is not true even in our own culture, let alone across more widely differing cultures.

Illusion drawings

2.4   You should have Art Sheets 1–4 from the Block 8 folder material in front of you while reading the remainder of this section. Illusion drawings are 'trick' drawings in the sense that they may lead us into using an inference habit where we should not, and so into making a wrong interpretation of the drawing. When this happens we are said to be *susceptible* to the illusion.

Activity 1
Illusion drawings
Allow about five minutes

Look at the four illusion drawings at the top of Art Sheet 1. For the Sander and Müller–Lyer figures, say which of the two purple lines you think is the longer; for each of the horizontal–vertical figures, say which of the two lines is the longer, the purple or the black. Check your answers with a ruler—even though you may think yourself familiar with these illusions, the particular versions shown here may still catch you out. A junior school child might be differently susceptible. (Explanation of your results is given throughout this section in the block.)

This is all very well but does it apply to children of diff. cultures born in this country.

2.5 If cultures differ in their perceptual inference habits, we might expect this to be reflected in susceptibility to different kinds of illusion, and two major studies, separated by half a century, have shown just this.

2.6 At the turn of this century, Dr W. H. R. Rivers accompanied the Cambridge Anthropological Expedition to the Torres Straits Islands (between Australia and New Guinea), where he collected a wide variety of perceptual data including the responses of some Murray Islanders to the Müller–Lyer and horizontal–vertical (H–V) illusions. A year later he studied the Todas, a small community in southern India, using the same illusions. For purposes of comparison, data was collected from English adults and children. On combining the results of his studies, Rivers found that the non-Western people he sampled were more susceptible to the H–V illusions than his English respondents, but that the reverse was true for the Müller–Lyer figure—although he apologetically noted à propos of his Torres Straits subjects that 'most of our observations on adults were made under the influence of tobacco'!

another useful anthrop. example

2.7 Rivers's findings of a bi-directional difference eliminated any simple explanation, such as the prevalent nineteenth-century view that 'primitive' people are less intelligent than 'civilized' people, and therefore they could be more easily and consistently duped by illusions. But it was left to Segall, Campbell and Herskovits, over fifty years later, to conceive a comprehensive hypothesis that might explain cultural differences in susceptibility to different illusions.

hypothesis

2.8 Segall *et al.* suggested that inference habits are based on the use of numerous 'cues' which are learned from the surrounding ecology, both natural (e.g. open savanna or dense rain forests) and cultural (i.e. the man-made artifacts in the environment such as buildings, books and utensils). Therefore, people with different environments would learn different—but always ecologically valid—visual inference habits, and hence be differently susceptible to various types of illusion. (See Art Sheet 1 for photos contrasting environmental cues.)

see it above. see this. Will children see this diff?

2.9 For the Müller–Lyer and Sander Parallelogram illusions, Segall, Campbell and Herskovits advanced the 'carpentered world' hypothesis. This states that in an environment replete with straight lines, right angles and rectangular objects (as in urban indoor environments in western societies) there will be a pervasive tendency learned early in life to interpret the acute and obtuse angles such objects project on the retina as right angles extended in space. Thus the Sander Parallelogram may be perceived as the representation of two rectangular surfaces extended in space, and the left diagonal is judged—wrongly—to be the longer because it *represents* a greater distance. Similarly, the Müller–Lyer figure may be perceived as representing a 3–D object extended in space—for example, the left horizontal as the back edge of a box, and the right horizontal as a front edge—so that the left appears to be longer, and the right shorter, than in the drawing.[1] Segall *et al.* predicted that Western people would be more susceptible to these illusions than people dwelling in uncarpentered environments who had little experience of two-dimensional line representations of 3–D objects.

carpentered world hypothesis

note over leaf: man who thought buffalo in distance were insects.

2.10 For the horizontal–vertical illusions, Segall *et al.* advanced a hypothesis based on the fact that, due to 'foreshortening', a fairly long line receding away from one in the horizontal plane gives rise to the same retinal image as a much shorter vertical line. They suggested that people living in flat, open environments would be most likely to develop the inference habit of compensating in length for the 'foreshortening' which occurs with such receding horizontals; and to use this habit when presented with the H–V illusions, i.e. to interpret their retinal image of the vertical line as a foreshortened horizontal line, and

foreshortening

[1]*Gregory (1966) reports a laboratory technique for measuring apparent depth which lends weight to Segall* et al.*'s hypothesis.*

Mention names as investigators in this area.

hence to interpret it as being longer than it really is in the drawing. Conversely, Segall *et al.* suggested that people living in restricted, 'vertical' environments, such as rain forests and canyon bottoms would be least likely to develop this inference habit—with city dwellers being kept from this extreme by the long, straight streets which divide dense areas of tall buildings. Thus Segall *et al.* predicted that plain dwellers living mainly outdoors would be most susceptible, groups living in urban areas moderately susceptible, and those living in restricted environments, least susceptible, to the H–V illusions.

2.11   Between 1956 and 1961, Segall, Campbell and Herskovits collected data from nearly 2,000 people in fifteen societies in the Philippines, the USA and many parts of Africa. They used several variations of the four illusion figures, each with a different discrepancy in the length of the two segments to be compared. Each time the respondent's task was to indicate the longer of the two segments (see Art Sheet 1). Data was also compiled on the natural and constructed environments of each society, as a way of assessing the extent of land and water vistas, the types of art forms, and the degree of rectangularity in dwellings, furnishings, tools, containers, etc.

2.12   The general trends of their results were as they had hypothesized (see Figure 1). Like Rivers, they found bi-directional differences for the two types of illusion. On the Müller–Lyer and Sander figures, their Western samples were significantly more susceptible to illusion than the non-Western samples, for whom rectangularity was relatively low and 2–D representational art rare. On the two horizontal–vertical illusions, the Western samples had medium scores, with some of the non-Western samples scoring significantly higher, and some lower, broadly in accordance with the openness of their environment. However, the overall fit of data to hypotheses is not very close, especially for the H–V illusions; nor could they demonstrate the precise position of each sample along a dimension measuring susceptibility to illusion. Campbell himself acknowledged that (1964, p. 316): 'If . . . ecology is a factor, as I do believe it is, it is obviously only one of many factors.'

Figure 1
Illusion susceptibility in European and non-European adult samples (from Segall et al., 1966, p. 149)

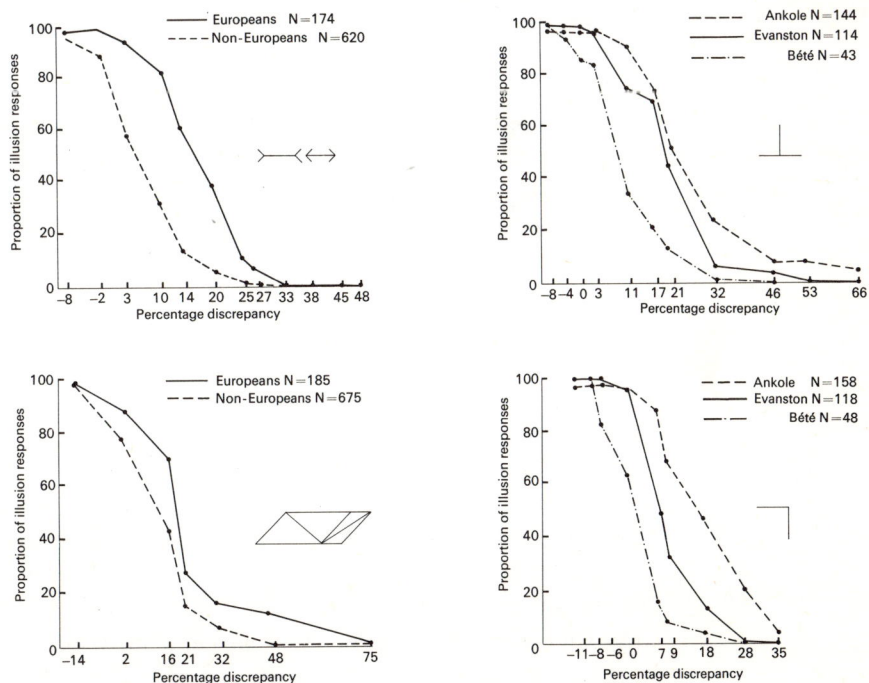

See over page for explanatory notes on Figure 1.

Notes on Figure 1

a   For the Müller–Lyer and Sander illusions, the combined results of all
non-European and European samples are shown. For the H–V illusions,
the results of three typical samples are shown, whose environments,
briefly, are as follows:

Ankole: open savanna (Uganda, Africa)
Bété: dense, compressed tropical forest (Ivory Coast, Africa)
Evanston: highly carpentered urban environment, lacking the extended
vistas of the savanna, but with frequent long flat streets (USA)

b   'Percentage discrepancy' is basically a quantification of illusion 'potency',
computed from actual and estimated discrepancies in the length of the two
segments to be compared. Each baseline point represents a different
version of the illusion concerned (see 2.11). The two segments are equal at
0 on the baseline. A negative percentage discrepancy indicates that the
typically overestimated segment is actually the longer of the two (but still
called, for convenience, an illusion response). When the percentage
discrepancy is large and positive, it is so much the shorter of the two that
the illusion rarely 'works'. As you can see, the bigger the positive percentage
discrepancy, the less susceptible all groups become—but some are
consistently more susceptible than others to all variations of the illusion.

2.13   The publication of Segall, Campbell and Herskovits's study aroused new
interest in illusion susceptibility, and since then several researchers have
taken up their hypotheses, with mixed results. While there has been some
qualified support for the ecological view (e.g. Gregor and McPherson, 1965),
on the whole attention has been directed towards other factors which may be
involved. Bonté (1962) found that differences in apparatus and method gave
rise to conflicting results, while Derogowski (1967) suggested that the ecological explanation really only fits the ⌐ version of the H–V illusion, and that
susceptibility to the ⊥ version has more to do with illusion effects produced by the dichosection of the horizontal line by the vertical. Similarly,
Jahoda (1966) found a purely ecological explanation to be inadequate for the
Müller–Lyer and Sander illusions. As you will remember, the 'carpentered
world' hypothesis included both degree of rectangularity in the environment
and experience in interpreting 2–dimensional drawings. Jahoda suggests that,
in fact, these should be treated as two distinct variables. He argues that the
individual's ability to interpret 2D drawings controls the extent to which
environmental rectangularity influences illusion susceptibility; and that, by
concentrating on global information about culture and ecology at the expense
of data about the experience of individual subjects, Segall *et al.* could only fail
to differentiate precisely between their non-European samples, even though
these varied in their degree of environmental regularity.

variable

sample

2.14   It seems clear from studies of illusion susceptibility that people from different
cultures do vary in their perceptual inference habits, but why they do so is still
a matter for debate. Most researchers have emphasized learning, and this is
supported by the fact that susceptibility changes with age. For example,
Western adults are less susceptible than children to the Müller–Lyer illusion,
a finding which Segall *et al.* explain thus: frequent childhood exposure to
pictures and drawings, and the resultant learning to interpret them, increases
susceptibility; later learning to *produce* 2–D representations (see Art Sheet 2),
decreases susceptibility. However, recent research (Jahoda 1971; Berry 1971)
has suggested that Müller–Lyer susceptibility may be partly related to retinal
pigmentation, which varies with age and also with skin colour. To date evidence on this point is conflicting, but if it was to become established, the
relation between physiology and learning in perception might need some
rethinking.

Nature–nurture

2.15   Nature–nurture apart, we need to know much more about classes of illusion if studies of them are to resolve the debate about the causes of different inference habits. The causes of inference habits are deduced from susceptibility to different classes of illusion; but unless illusion drawings are correctly classified, susceptibility may be attributed to the wrong cause. (This is exactly what Deregowski suggests Segall *et al.* did, in classifying both the ⌐ and ⊥ versions of the H–V illusion together under the ecological/foreshortening hypothesis.) But even if illusion studies cannot yet satisfactorily answer questions about 'why' there are cultural differences in perception, they do at least provide a beginning to our knowledge of 'who sees what and under which conditions'. Depth perception has been shown to be an important factor in illusion susceptibility, and it is to this we now turn in more detail.

Depth perception and representational art

2.16   The Western 'perspective' art style consists basically of a set of geometric rules for producing 2–D representations that will generate, as nearly as possible, the same retinal images as the actual objects would generate. It is hard for us as Westerners to realize that while the *rules* of perspective drawing are non-arbitrary, the *decision* to represent things this way is an arbitrary cultural convention. This point is amplified in Art Sheet 3, which samples the variety of representational conventions across cultures and over time. It is irrelevant to consider whether one style is 'better' or 'worse' than another, for each has its own techniques and purposes. The things to bear in mind are firstly that with any technique there is a triple reality—the actual patches of colour on a flat surface, the representation the viewer perceives, and the representation the artist intends. And secondly, the fact that some people may not see depth in perspective drawings does not preclude their seeing depth in other styles of representation, or in actuality.

Figure 2
Pictorial depth perception in sub-cultural groups in Africa (from Hudson, 1960, p. 186)

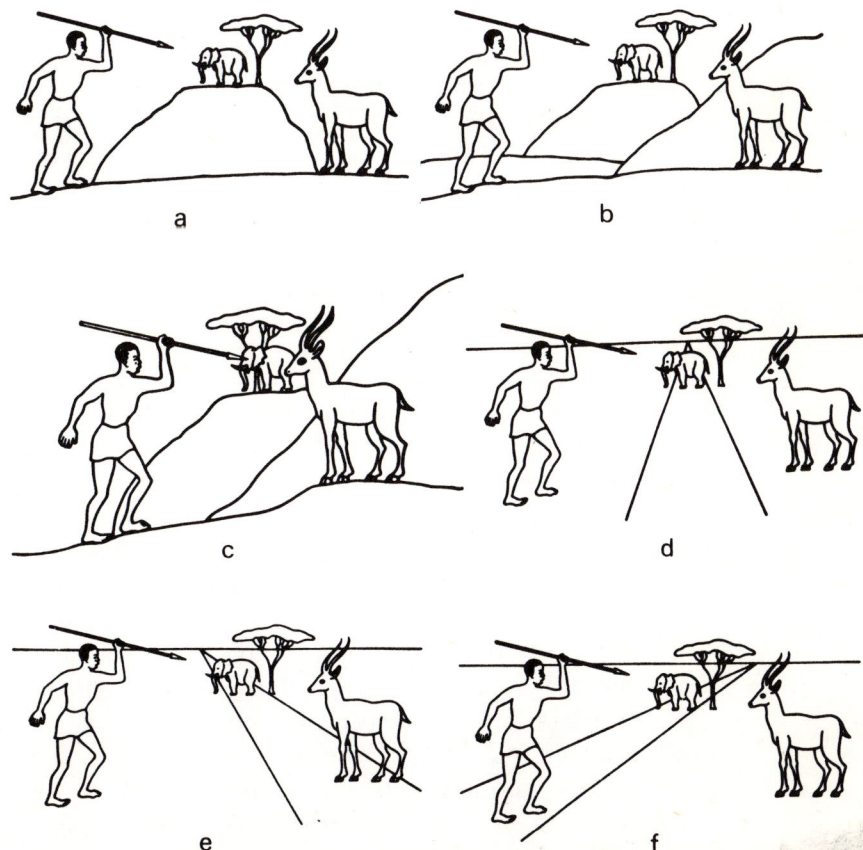

2.17   Extensive research has been carried out by W. Hudson in South Africa into the relationship between culture, education and 3–D perception (Hudson,

1960, 1967). For part of his work, Hudson devised a series of six outline drawings which are differently interpreted according to whether or not the viewer takes account of the depth cues in them (e.g. object size, overlap and perspective). In each picture (see Figure 2) the hunter's spear is aligned on both elephant and antelope: the 3–D viewer says, 'correctly', that the hunter is aiming at the antelope; the 2–D viewer that he is aiming at the elephant. Hudson tested ten groups of subjects by asking them for each picture: 'What do you see?' 'What is the man doing?' 'Which is nearer the man—the elephant or the antelope?' His results are summarized in Table 1.

Table 1   Summary of Hudson's results (from Hudson, 1960, Table 4 adapted)

Sample	N[1]	Education	% 3–D subjects*	Cultural description
1: Black mine labourers	57	none	0	'Isolated, migratory, rurally orientated'
2: Black mine labourers	54	ex-primary	0	
3: Black mine clerks	48	ex-secondary	26	
4: White labourers	60	ex-primary	15	'Isolated and inward looking; sheltered employment'
5: White schoolchildren	42	primary beginners	36	(no description; implied as cultural norm)
6: White schoolchildren	32	primary finishers	86	
7: White schoolchildren	113	all primary standards	61	
8: Black schoolchildren	34	secondary beginners	60	'First generation urban-dwellers; ethnocentrically isolated.'
9: Black schoolchildren	52	secondary seniors	72	
10: Black teachers	25	graduates	67	

*Percentage of subjects making 3–D responses, averaged over all six drawings.

2.18   Responses to the question 'what do you see?' gave related evidence of depth cues being misperceived. 2–D viewers saw the outline of the hill as a path, or letters of the alphabet. A few rejected their 2–D perception on the logical grounds that a hunter would never attack an elephant with only a spear, while some of the graduates asked for guidance because they could see the pictures both flat and in depth.

2.19   For the white primary samples (5–7) it appeared that 3–D perception was associated with educational level. But the same conclusion did not hold for the black pupils (8–10), who were at a higher educational level but performing less well than the white upper-primary children. Amongst the working samples (1–4) also, educational level appeared to make little impact in terms of increased 3–D perception. Training in pictorial perception was not included in the formal African school curriculum, although exposure to pictures occurred, and so Hudson looked to cultural influences outside the school. As you can see from Table 1, he described samples 1–4 and 8–10 as culturally isolated from the white Westernized norm. One aspect of this isolation is a lack of perspective pictorial material in the home, in contrast to samples 5–7 who receive almost continuous informal exposure to books, magazines, photos etc. Other cultural differences which he considered were the non-perspective nature of indigenous African art, and the possibility that in the past auditory perception may have developed at the expense of visual

[1]N is the standard way of representing number.

perception in his black samples, and vice-versa for his white samples.[1]

2.20   Hudson concluded that while educational level was a factor in the development of pictorial depth perception, it could be overriden by cultural experiences of the sort described above. This conclusion has been challenged by Dawson (1967) who, as you will see in Section 3, has suggested that field-dependence may be the major limiting factor in the development of depth perception. Other research has shown that depth perception depends more on the specific stimulus or task than Hudson supposed. For example, Deregowski (1972) reports that African adults from relatively pictureless environments can nevertheless recognize *familiar* objects in photographs. He also found that many of the Zambian schoolboys and adults who made '2–D responses' on Hudson's test could build 3–D models from line drawings. Equally Jahoda and McGurk (1974) found no significant differences between African, European and Chinese schoolchildren on a similar type of construction task, although they noted (as have Hudson and others) that the children found linear perspective more difficult to understand than the depth cues of object size and overlap.

*field-dependence/
independence
limiting factor*

2.21   Although African difficulties with pictorial depth perception may not be as acute as could be supposed from the results of Hudson's test alone, nevertheless there is sufficient evidence to suggest that some caution should be exercised in using visual aids and pictorial material in educational and test situations. African schooling is still, generally, very formal, emphasizing verbal rote learning. Incidental exposure to pictures in this context is unlikely to overcome the very real problems often found, for example, when using illustrated textbooks from Britain or America. The need for training in perception, and in handling and organizing visual and spatial materials is now recognized, and as more becomes known about specific difficulties and about how we translate 2–D into 3–D, the more effective such programmes should become (see 2.23).

2.22   Meanwhile a cautionary tale is provided by the account in Art Sheet 4 of Hudson's research into the effectiveness of safety education posters for Bantu factory workers. This research brings home the three themes of Art Sheets 3 and 4. Firstly, the viewer's interpretation of a drawing—whether it is an illusion figure, a hunting scene, or a safety poster—is highly dependent on the particular knowledge and experience he brings to it. Secondly, with representations of reality, familiarity with the particular set of rules and techniques—the code if you like—used by the image-maker is critical to the viewer's understanding. And thirdly, the viewer's interpretation of a picture may be influenced by words accompanying it. Art Sheet 2, which you may like to consider at this point, is concerned with two aspects of drawings specifically by children: the development of perspective art skill in children from our own culture, and Wayne Dennis's cross-cultural research into the social values revealed in children's drawings of men.

Allied perceptual difficulties

2.23   Several researchers have found that Africans may experience difficulties with materials such as jigsaws and pattern completion tests designed to assess their ability to manipulate spatial relations. However, a small experiment by McFie (1961) suggests that such difficulties may be overcome with suitable training. He gave twenty-six teenage Ugandan boys entering technical training school a battery of perceptual-spatial tests, which included Kohs Blocks, pictures to describe and designs to remember. Scores on these tests increased

*Kohs Blocks design
test*

---

[1]*See also 3.13 where there is some support for this hypothesis, although it is unclear
whether this difference is genetic as Hudson implies. Sample 4's results are at variance
with this hypothesis, and Hudson offers the questionable explanation that their results are
due to a combination of cultural isolation and genetic inferiority in general intelligence.*

significantly on retesting two years later; performance was faster and spatial orientation far more accurate. McFie suggested that this was due to the boys' experience in handling and studying physical objects, and stressed again the need for less purely verbal learning and more practical activities to be included in the African school curricula. (A similar shift of emphasis in the curriculum is to be seen in Television Programme 12, *Education in Trinidad*.)

2.24   As you may remember from Block 5 (Cognitive Styles), a rather special form of perceptual-spatial ability is the ability to separate figure from ground, which Witkin termed field-dependence/independence. In the next section, cross-cultural evidence relating to Witkin's findings will be considered. At this point you may wish to stop and refresh your memory with the correspondence text of Block 5, or the article by Witkin, 'Some implications of research on cognitive style for problems of education' (p. 288 in the first volume of the Reader)[1].

3 Socialization and field-independence

3.1   Field-independence is the ability to perceive items as separate from their context. It forms a continuum from complete dependence, where items are experienced as fused with the ground, to complete independence. But most people fall between these two extremes. Extensive research by Witkin and his associates in the USA has suggested that individuals differ consistently in their tendency to separate and differentiate in their perception, thinking and personal characteristics such as body concept and sense of separate identity. Witkin sees these differences as diverse expressions of an underlying process of personality development which he calls psychological differentiation, and his research has linked them with different patterns of mother–child interaction.

psychological differentiation

3.2   As Witkin himself notes (1967, p. 102), these patterns of interaction are in turn related to the nature of the physical environment. Environments vary in the degree to which they are naturally differentiated (contrast English countryside with the Sahara desert, for example), but such differences are not in themselves so important. What *is* important is that they appear to dictate socialization practices insofar as certain personality traits and skills are needed for survival in a given environment. This point is illustrated by Barry, Child and Bacon's study (1959) of socialization practices and personality traits in societies with subsistence economies. They suggested that, to best meet their economic needs, adults in societies where the environment permits only low food accumulation (e.g. fishing or hunting) should tend to be 'individualistic, assertive and venturesome'. In contrast, adults in societies where the environment permits high food accumulation (e.g. agricultural or pastoral peoples) should tend to be 'conscientious, compliant and conservative'. Ratings for 104 societies of the degree of food accumulation and of six aspects of socialization (training in obedience, responsibility, nurturance, achievement, self-reliance and general independence) upheld their predictions. They were able to show a significant relationship between the type of subsistence economy of a society, the socialization practices it used, and personality characteristics.

subsistence economies

---

[1]*Whitehead, J. M. (ed.) (1975)* Personality and Learning 1, *London, Hodder and Stoughton/The Open University Press.*

correlation

3.3   The main concern of this section is with perceptual field-independence and its ecological and social correlates, rather than with the wider aspects of Witkin's theory. Three studies are presented, which not only replicate some of Witkin's research, but also extend it in rather different ways. The first study, by Dawson, links pictorial depth perception with field-independence. The second, by Wober, challenges Witkin's claim that an individual's level of field-independence is consistent across all sense modalities. The third, by Berry, provides a functional model for exploring the interactions between ecology, culture and individual behaviour, which he illustrates with a study of the adaptation of child-rearing practices and perceptual-spatial skills to ecological pressures.

sense modalities

3.4   Each study is followed by an activity designed to help you judge the research for yourself. The questions raised relate back to the purposes of cross-cultural research outlined earlier (1.11), viz. what variations in cognitive functioning are found in cultures very different from Western ones, and what causes them? Can Witkin's concept of field-independence be considered universal (i.e. is his theory likely to hold true in all cultures)? What light do such studies shed on the forces that shape cognitive development in our own culture? One aim of *Personality and Learning* is to help you consider research findings carefully and critically, and this section is included partly for that purpose. You may find it helpful to refer to the Methodology Handbook at certain points.

A study of Temne and Mende, by Dawson

3.5   Dawson's study of field-independence in the Temne and Mende, two tribes in Sierra Leone, arose from his dissatisfaction with Hudson's conclusion that cultural isolation from the Westernized norm was the critical factor in African difficulties with pictorial depth perception. In particular, he queried Hudson's assessment of the graduate teachers (Sample 10, Table 1) as lacking sufficient contact with the cultural norm, despite their many years of education and experience in an urban, carpentered environment.

3.6   Dawson therefore formed a different hypothesis. He accepted that education, environment, and cultural isolation were relevant to the development of pictorial depth perception up to a certain point, but went on to suggest that the crucial limiting factor would be socialization practices which promoted a less analytic, more field-dependent perceptual style. Such a style he argued, could be expected to limit the acquisition of other perceptual-spatial skills—such as making use of depth cues to perceive pictorial material in three dimensions.

3.7   Dawson specifically chose to study the Temne and Mende tribes because they differ in socialization practices in ways which, on the basis of Witkin's studies, led him to expect a contrast in field-independence, the Mende being relatively field-independent, and the Temne relatively field-dependent. According to social anthropological literature, the Temne child is subject to severe discipline after weaning. Great stress is placed on his conforming to adult authority, and extreme physical punishment is often used to enforce this. Children are not encouraged to adopt an adult role. Individual competition is also discouraged, and group reliance is developed through the use of harsh social sanctions, such as 'swears' and 'accusations of witchcraft' against those who deviate from tribal norms. In addition, the Temne mother plays a dominant role in child-rearing, because the polygamous family group means that other wives and children occupy much of the father's time.

social sanctions

tribal norms
polygamy

3.8   The Mende present a contrasting picture in a number of these characteristics. Punishment is less frequent, and more likely to take the form of deprivation rather than physical control. Individual initiative is encouraged, and the child is given responsibility at an early age. The Mende family is less dominated by the mother, and parents are more consistent than the Temne in their child-rearing behaviour. Thus the Temne and Mende differ considerably in opportunities for the child to separate from the mother and to develop his own internalized standards—the two socialization factors which Witkin identifies in his article, in the first volume of the Reader, as affecting field-dependence/independence.

Embedded Figures Test

3.9   To assess field-independence, Dawson used a specially modified version of the Embedded Figures Test (EFT), and the Kohs Block Design Test, which is recognized by Witkin as a measure of field-independence. For depth perception he used two of Hudson's drawings (cf. Figure 2) and six more of his own, which also contained the depth cues of object size, overlap and perspective. As in Hudson's procedure, subjects were asked to identify the objects in the pictures and then to say which of a number of objects was closer in distance to another object. They were also asked to rate each of their parents as 'very strict', 'fairly strict' or 'not so strict' as a means of assessing child-rearing practices. Subjects were all adult males with good vision and of similar age (20–24 years), education (Form I, secondary), occupation (skilled workers), and intelligence[1].

3.10   Dawson's results are summarized in Tables 2 and 3. Table 2 is concerned with the relationship of pictorial depth perception to other variables.

Table 2   Correlation matrix (Sierra Leone male sample, N = 99) (from Dawson, 1967, p. 120, Table 2)

	Educ.	SL2 Intell.	Kohs Blocks	EFT	3–D
Education	–	.37	.21	.20	.22
Intelligence SL2	.37	–	.52	.43	.41
Kohs Blocks	.21	.52	–	.73	.64
EFT	.20	.43	.73	–	.66
3–D	.22	.41	.64	.66	–

A correlation of .20 is significant at the .05 level with a sample of this size, 99.

Pictorial version of Table 3

---

[1]*That is, scoring similarly on one particular intelligence test, the SL2 (SL = Sierra Leone) group test. Dawson describes this test as 'constructed in terms of the indigenous culture'. Section 6 will consider intelligence testing.*

Table 3   Temne and Mende categories of maternal strictness and mean scores on perceptual tests (from Dawson, 1967, p. 124, Table 5 adapted)

Categories of maternal strictness	Temne subjects: mean scores				Mende subjects: mean scores			
	N	3–D	Kohs Blocks	EFT	N	3–D	Kohs Blocks	EFT
Mother very strict	22	0.9	9.9	21.9	9	3.7	13.1	39.9
Mother fairly strict	18	4.9	19.9	90.1	20	4.7	20.8	87.1
Mother not so strict	8	4.0	20.9	55.9	21	3.5	17.9	84.6
Probability that the differences between the three mean scores could have arisen by chance.*	p	0.05	0.01	0.001		ns	0.05	0.05

*Analysis like this is discussed in the Methodology Handbook in the section on analysis of variance. The example there is concerned with three teaching methods in place of the three categories of maternal strictness in this Table. Both probabilities are based on the F-statistic.

Table 3 shows the relationship between socialization practices, field-independence and pictorial depth perception. Dawson also carried out a 3–D teaching experiment to test the hypothesis that '2–D subjects' could be taught to perceive pictorial material in depth, but only within the limits of their field-independence scores. Twenty-four Temne males were initially tested for field-independence (Kohs Blocks) and 3–D perception, and a matched study group and a control group were set up. The study group was then taught how to produce and interpret 3–D representations in 8 one-hour weekly sessions. Both groups were retested for 3–D perception three months later, and the result is shown in Table 4. Note that scores in Tables 3 and 4 are mean scores. Low scores on Kohs and EFT indicate greater field-dependence; similarly, low 3–D scores indicate more two-dimensional performance.

Table 4   3–D pictorial perception teaching experiment (from Dawson, 1967, p. 126, Table 7)

Sample	N	3–D pictorial perception first test (June 1961)	3–D pictorial perception second test (Dec. 1961)
Study group mean scores	12	0.50	3.83
Control group mean scores	12	0.17	0.50
Significance level (probability of the difference between the two groups in 3–D scores on retesting being due to chance): p = 0.001			

rank order correlation

Rank order correlation (an index of the extent to which subjects hold the same rank position on two tests) for members of the Study group on initial Kohs testing (3.10) and second 3–D test: ρ = 0.884, which is significant at the 0.001 level.

Activity 2	**Q1**	'The stricter the mother the more field-dependent the child.' Decide whether Table 3 supports this proposition by considering:

Activity 2
Temne and Mende
field-independence
Allow about twenty minutes

Q1 'The stricter the mother the more field-dependent the child.' Decide whether Table 3 supports this proposition by considering:

a   the Kohs and EFT scores for Temne subjects with mothers of different grades of strictness.

b   the Kohs and EFT scores for Mende subjects with mothers of different grades of strictness.

c   how the Temne and Mende compare on their scores and the general pattern of maternal strictness.

If you consider the proposition to be only partly supported, give your reason.

Q2 Dawson claims that he has found 'considerable evidence . . . that the acquisition of perceptual skills is limited by the field-dependence variable'.

a   what are the relationships between measures of 3–D perception and field-independence in Tables 2 and 4 which support this claim?

b   does the pattern of scores in Table 3 (this time considering the Kohs and EFT scores in relation to the 3–D scores) also support this claim?

Discussion of Activity 2

Q1 On the following grounds the proposition is in my view, only partially supported.

a   *Temne:* On the Kohs Blocks Test, sons of the strictest mothers produce scores with the lowest mean (i.e. are most field dependent); sons of 'fairly strict' mothers score intermediately, and the sons of the least ('not so') strict mothers produce scores with the highest mean (i.e. are least field-dependent). This is as Dawson predicted. However, on the EFT, while sons of 'very strict' mothers again produce the lowest mean, the mean scores of the 'not-so-strict' and 'fairly strict' groups are the reverse of what would be expected.

b   *Mende*: On both Kohs Blocks and the EFT, subjects with 'very strict' mothers again have the lowest mean score, indicating that they are the most field-dependent. But this time, on both tests, the mean scores of the 'not-so-strict' and 'fairly strict' groups are reversed.

c   *Temne and Mende compared*: The distribution of mothers by category of strictness is significantly different in the two tribes. The literature suggests that the Mende are less strict than the Temne, and this is supported by the higher Mende means on Kohs Blocks and EFT for sons of 'very strict' mothers. The 'fairly strict' groups show little difference in means, as do the 'not-so-strict' groups, on Kohs Blocks at least—but, as we have seen, these two categories of strictness are associated with some rather curious results in both Temne and Mende.

Part of the problem seems to me to lie with the use of subjective assessments of maternal strictness. Although Dawson says the meaning of the categories was explained, this does not preclude different interpretations both within and between tribes. It is of note that Berry (1966) decided, in his first study of field-independence and socialization in the Temne and Eskimo, to abandon Dawson's three categories in favour of a straightforward division 'more' or 'less' strict, because subjects were obviously responding in an 'all or none' fashion. Moreover, although the sorts of socialization differences which Witkin considers important are evident in the literature on the two tribes, it is arguable whether 'strictness' best summarizes them.

correlation

Q2 Table 2 shows that although the 3–D test correlates significantly with education and intelligence, its highest correlations are with the measures of field-independence (Kohs and EFT). Stronger evidence comes from Table 4, where although the Study Groups' 3–D performance on retesting had significantly improved over that of the control group, (which showed only practice effects), the members of the Study Group retained nearly the same rank positions ($\rho = .884$) as they had held on Kohs, the original measure of field-independence, i.e. 3–D performance may have improved, but still appears very much related to field-dependence; 'limited' by it in Dawson's words. However, in Table 3, 3–D means only partially follow the pattern of strictness and field-dependence—which is, as I said above, not entirely clear in itself.

myelination

3.11   Dawson was also concerned with the effects on the development of field-independence of the protein-deficiency disease Kwashiorkor—a Ghanaian word meaning 'the sickness an older child gets when the next child is born' (and by implication he loses his mother's milk). As a result of poverty and/or ignorance of the infant's need for protein, Kwashiorkor is widespread in Africa. It affects myelination (Block 4, Sections 5.32–5.34) and also the functioning of the liver; the latter may result for males in Gynaecomastia, a hormonal disturbance leading to a degree of physiological feminization.

3.12   As you read in Block 5, Section 3.16, Witkin found females to be on average slightly more field-dependent than males. Using a sample of 150 mine apprentices, ten of whom had Gynaecomastia, Dawson showed that greater field-dependence was associated with physiological feminization, which he also suggested gave rise to more 'feminine' interests and greater susceptibility to maternal domination and social sanctions. Berry's research with Eskimos raises again the question of the relation between biological and social causes of field-dependence. But meanwhile let us look at some research by Wober on a rather different aspect of Witkin's work.

A comparison of Nigerian and American sense modalities, by Wober

proprioceptive sense

3.13   Wober's research into field-independence stems from his interest in the way different cultures stress different senses in communication. Wober suggests that while the visual world provides the currency of communication in Western societies, in African cultures the auditory and proprioceptive (body sensitivity) senses may be more important. Many West African languages—including those in Nigeria—are tonal[1], and feeling for rhythm and tone is well developed. Babies learn to walk and dance at a very early age, and dancing and physical expression are extremely important elements of these cultures. To express the differential development of the senses, Wober coined the term 'sensotype', which he defined as 'the pattern of relative importance of the different senses, by which a child learns to perceive the world and in which pattern he develops his abilities'.[2]

Rod and Frame Test

3.14   All Witkin's tests of field-independence (see Block 5, Section 3.5–3.18) require the analysis of visual information, but the Rod and Frame Test (RFT) also involves analysis of proprioceptive information. Witkin used the significant correlations between the EFT and RFT that he found with his American subjects (Block 5, Section 3.13, Table 6) to support his hypothesis that these tests are tapping a generalized ability to separate figure from context which is consistent across senses. But Wober suggested that this consistency only occurs because visual and proprioceptive senses are equally developed (although not equally used) in Western cultures. He hypothesized that in cultures where, as in Nigeria, the evidence suggests that proprioceptivity is more dominant than visuality in the cultural sensotype, test performance

[1]*i.e. words may retain the same phonemes and spelling for quite different meanings, the difference being made clear in speech by the tone or pitch of different syllables, and in writing by the context (or sometimes, signs like accents for learners). In Igbo, the language of the Nigerian Ibo, for example, 'akwa' can mean egg, crying, cloth, bed or bridge, according to the way it is said.*

[2]*Wober notes that, cultural experience aside, sensory defects may also be responsible for the development of different sensotypes. For example, it is widely acknowledged that the blind develop more acute hearing than the sighted, and Witkin himself has found that congenitally blind subjects perform better than subjects with sight on aural field independence tests.*

would reflect this differential development of the senses. In other words, field-independence might be specific to particular senses, rather than a necessarily generalized ability.

3.15   Wober's subjects were 173 skilled and unskilled manual workers from a large Nigerian industry, with varying levels of Western education. They came from the Ibo and Edo tribal groups, both of which have evolved cultures lacking literacy but with intense development of music, dancing and tonal language. Both groups have had similar exposure to Western influences. The tests used were the RFT (eighty-eight subjects only), Raven's Matrices (see Block 5, Figure 13), and shortened forms of the EFT and Kohs Blocks.

Raven's Matrices

3.16   Wober's results are summarized in Tables 5 and 6. Table 5 shows Nigerian results on the RFT and compares them with earlier American data from Witkin and Asch (1948). Table 6 is a correlation matrix, showing the relationships between Nigerian test performance, education and job efficiency.

Table 5   Nigerian and American RFT scores (from Wober, 1967, Tables 1 and 2 adapted)

Frame position	Chair and body position	Nigerian mean score*	American mean score*
Straight	Tilted	1.25	4.53
Tilted	Straight	11.33	5.95

*Score = mean degrees subject displaced rod from true vertical

Table 6   Nigerian correlations between scores on field-independence tests and other variables (from Wober, 1966, Table 6.3, p. 123)

	RFT	EFT	Kohs Blocks	Raven's Matrices	Education	Job efficiency	N
RFT	–	.18[a]	.16[a]	.19[a]	.04[a]	.26	88
EFT	.18[a]	–	.63	.51	.47	.07[a]	173
Kohs	.16[a]	.63	–	.53	.38	.06[a]	173
Raven's	.19[a]	.51	.53	–	.30	−0.13[a]	173
Education	.04[a]	.47	.38	.30	–	−0.05[a]	173
Efficiency	.26	.07[a]	.06[a]	−0.13[a]	−0.05[a]	–	173

Note: For N = 88, 0.05 significance arises when p = 0.2; for N = 173, 0.05 significance arises when p = 0.1
[a]Values of p not significant

Author's note: Remember Witkin found significant correlations between results on EFT and RFT with his American subjects (Block 5, Table 6)

**Activity 3
Nigerian and American sense modalities**
Allow about twenty minutes

Q1   In the Rod and Frame Test, which type of sensory information is more prominent when:

a   the frame is tilted, but the chair and body are straight?
b   the frame is straight, but the chair and body are tilted?

Q2   'Wober's research provides evidence for a Nigerian sensotype that differs from the Western one.'
a   How does the data in Table 5 (differences in scores on the RFT) and Table 6 (correlations between RFT and EFT) support this statement?
b   What are the implications for Witkin's concept of field-dependence/independence?

Q3   **Consider the correlations in Table 6 between education and EFT, Kohs Blocks and Raven's Matrices, and the correlation between education and RFT. What do they suggest about the role of education in Nigeria in fostering the development of field-independence?**

Q4   **In our own culture, what sort of sensotype does our education system encourage? What of the new media now widely available (TV, tape, radio, records, etc)?**

Discussion of Activity 3

Q1   a   visual

     b   proprioceptive (although still a visual element)

Q2   a   Table 5 shows that the Nigerians scored better when proprioceptivity was important (i.e. frame straight/chair and body tilted), both relative to American scores on that condition, and relative to their own scores, when the test was dependent on visuality (i.e. the frame tilted/chair and body straight condition, where their errors were ten times as large). In contrast, the difference in American scores on the two conditions was small. Table 6 shows no significant correlation between Nigerian EFT and RFT results, in contrast to Witkin's findings in America. This also implies that the development of analytic competence in the visual and proprioceptive senses follows a different pattern in Nigeria compared with America.

     b   Wober's findings suggest that Witkin may be incorrect to think of field-independence as a generalized ability in the individual. This is not to say that the concept of field-dependence/independence has no validity in the cross-cultural context; rather, that it may need to be modified to allow for differential sensory emphasis and development in different cultures. Further research is really needed to confirm this possibility.

Q3   Education is significantly related to EFT, Kohs Blocks and Raven's Matrices, suggesting that it fosters the development of purely visual field-independence. The RFT, on the other hand, is not significantly related to formal education, reinforcing the notion that 'proprioceptive field-independence' is developed specifically by the Nigerian cultures.

Q4   Apart from specialist provision (e.g. for musicians and dancers), our present education system only appears to develop visual skills relating to literacy.

     Wober's concept of sensotype as related to cultural modes of communication (visual/auditory/proprioceptive) has an interesting parallel in the ideas of Marshall McLuhan. McLuhan is concerned with the relationship in Western cultures between the senses and styles of communication based on different technologies. He contrasts the conventional, 'hot', medium of print which 'anaesthetizes' all the senses except the visual, with the newer, 'cold', electronic media which make new calls on the senses and on memory. (Take the example of TV, which has only recently become a dominant factor in the lives of children—and adults. We are only beginning to find out what influence it has on people, about using it as a teaching and learning medium, and about teaching the uses of it to children and adults.)

     In a controversial paper, Postman (1970) argues that when a new communications technology enters a culture and becomes widely available, it not only generates new patterns of sensing and communication but 'consequently releases tremendous energies and causes people to seek new ways of organizing their institutions'. He considers the impact of the printing press, and then writes of the new electronic media:

> It's worth saying that the gurus of the peace movement—Bob Dylan, Pete Seeger, Joan Baez, Phil Ochs, for instance—were known to their constituency mostly as voices on LP records. It's worth saying that Vietnam, being our first television war, is also the most unpopular war in

our history. It's worth saying that Lyndon Johnson was the first president ever to have resigned because of a 'credibility gap'. . . Electronic media are predictably working to unloose disruptive social and political ideas, along with new forms of sensibility and expression. Whether this is being achieved by the structure of the media, or by their content, or by some combination of both, we cannot be sure. But like Gutenberg's infernal machine of 450 years ago, the electric plug is causing all hell to break loose. Meanwhile the schools are still pushing the old technology. . .

A study of Temne and Eskimo, by Berry

3.17   The final study in this section is described in the article by J. W. Berry (1971) 'Ecological and cultural factors in spatial perceptual development' (pp. 112–123 in the second volume of the Reader)[1]. Although Berry talks about 'visual-spatial skill development' rather than 'field-independence' he uses the same tests as those used in other studies of field-independence and, like Witkin, he is concerned with the relationship between socialization and the degree of visual differentiation. He takes Witkin's theory a step further by demonstrating how socialization practices vary systematically with other environmental and cultural (language and arts/crafts development) differences. Berry argues that socialization practices, language and arts/crafts must all be seen as *cultural mediators* between the environment and the development of visual differentiation. As he points out elsewhere (Berry, 1966, p. 212), the mere fact that the land requires certain skills is no guarantee that such skills will automatically develop—migration to less demanding territory or extinction are two possible alternatives. Hence his model of behaviour as *adaptive* to cultural characteristics, which are in turn *adaptive* to the 'demands' or 'pressures' which the physical environment places on people. ('Adaptation' itself does not imply progress or regress, although we may choose to place such values on the process.) You should now read the article by Berry. Allow fifty minutes for reading since, although it is quite short, Berry's argument is densely presented.

Reading
Ecological and cultural factors in spatial perceptual development
Berry (1971)
Reader 2, pp. 112–123

Activity 4
Factors in spatial perceptual development
Allow about twenty-five minutes

Q1   **On the basis of information in Berry's article, especially the data in Figures 2–5, describe briefly the ecology of the Temne Mayola, the cultural characteristics which may be inferred from their ecological rank order, and their visual-spatial abilities.**

Q2   **How do the traditional and transitional samples differ in test performance? What might account for the difference?**

Q3   **In what terms does Berry actually define 'ecology'? How adequately do you think his concept of 'ecological demand' explains the level of spatial-perceptual skill development for all types of groups in his study?**

Q4   **What are the implications for our culture of Dawson and Berry's findings concerning male–female levels of field-independence?**

Discussion of Activity 4

geo-spatial linguistic distinctions

Q1   The Mayola are a high-food accumulating society, where little or no hunting is done. Since Berry says rank orderings on 'cultural mediators' were identical with ecological rank orderings, we can infer severe socialization practices, little art/craft development and few geo-spatial linguistic distinctions. High scores on the visual discrimination test and low scores on Kohs, EFT and Raven's Matrices indicate a relatively small degree of perceptual differentiation.

Q2   The transitional samples have lower 'discrimination' means, and higher Kohs, EFT and Matrices means, than their partner traditional samples, indicating a greater degree of perceptual differentiation. Berry suggests that even though hunting activity is likely to have diminished for the transitional samples, this change is more than compensated for by the introduction of Western education, especially literacy. It might also be that the visual-spatial skills under study are only partly equivalent to those needed for survival by the traditional samples, whereas they are skills typically relevant to the Western cultures in which the tests were devised and with which, by definition, the transitional groups have had more contact.

Q3   As you probably realized when answering Q1, Berry's definition of ecology is not directly in terms of the physical environment but in *'the degree of food accumulation and its concomitant, the presence of hunting'*. Certain facts about soil, climate, plant and animal life (and hence population density and settlement pattern) are thus implied.

In the case of traditional hunting peoples, such as the Eskimo, where the environment will only permit one type of food-gathering, the ecological demand for high spatial-perceptual skills seems clear and unambiguous. But Berry's definition of ecology purely in terms of food-gathering techniques rather begs the question of why, in environments which will support, say, both hunting and agriculture (presumably like that of the Temne), does one type of food-gathering predominate? Berry (in press) only writes: 'in the bulk of those societies inhabiting areas where cultivation is possible, various forms of agriculture are pursued; without implying that this form of economic exploitation is higher or more advanced, it is indeed the case that where it is possible, societies produce or grow their food rather than gathering or chasing it.' Although Berry found that the level of spatial-perceptual skill corresponded with his 'ecological rank ordering' of the groups, it is debatable whether ecological demand alone is sufficient to explain why this should be so. Certainly Western education, as well as ecological demand, appears to influence the level of skill in the transitional samples. Since writing the article printed in Reader 2, Berry (in press) has considerably refined his original model of the interactions between ecology, culture and individual behaviour to include more explicitly culture contact and change.

Q4   Dawson alerts us to the fact that hormonal differences may play a part in differences in field-independence both within and between the sexes, while Berry stresses that when visual-spatial skills are reasonably developed, greater female field-dependence arises only when male–female role separation is strong, as in our society. While accepting an inevitable interaction between biological and social forces, we are at least in a position to try to alter the latter if we so choose!

role separation

4 Language as a mould to thought?

4.1   Language is one of the most obvious areas in which cultures differ. Intuitively, it seems quite reasonable to suppose that people with markedly different languages will, as a result, think in rather different ways about the world. But do they? In this section we shall consider the evidence for such a proposition—which is, in fact, commonly called the *Whorfian hypothesis*. Formulated in the 1920s and 1930s by two American linguists, Edward Sapir and Benjamin Lee Whorf, this hypothesis comprises two principles:

a   *Linguistic determinism*—the assertion that language determines our cognition, provides the mould in which our thoughts are cast, and dictates the way in which we organize and analyse the external world.

b   *Linguistic relativity*—the further assertion, with determinism taken as given, that people whose languages differ widely (in phonemes, lexicon and grammar) do not as a consequence merely have different labels for the same world, but will hold fundamentally different world views.

4.2   The Whorfian hypothesis, and related research, are not so much something new, as attempts to restate scientifically and evaluate objectively, ideas about linguistic relativity that have occurred for centuries in folklore and early science. Long ago the Ancient Greeks applied the term 'barbarian' (those who say 'ba-ba') to unfortunate foreigners denied the gift of Greek by the gods, **ethnolinguistics** while nineteenth century ethnolinguists busily began to catalogue differences between languages in grammar and vocabulary, following Wilhelm von Humboldt's pronouncement that: 'Man lives with the world about him principally, indeed . . . exclusively, as language presents it'.

4.3   In some circles the Whorfian hypothesis has fallen into disrepute, partly because like Freudian theory, it is difficult to test empirically. But again like Freudian theory, some researchers, rather than dismissing it, have attempted to delimit more clearly which aspects of the theory hold good, and under which conditions. We shall consider some of their findings shortly, but first the following article by Whorf outlines his thinking in more detail.

Reading

Science and Linguistics
Abridged from Whorf (1940)

Every normal person in the world, past infancy in years, can and does talk. By virtue of that fact, every person—civilized or uncivilized—carries through life certain naïve but deeply rooted ideas about talking and its relation to thinking. Because of their firm connection with speech habits that have become unconscious and automatic, these notions tend to be rather intolerant of opposition. They are by no means entirely personal and haphazard; their basis is definitely systematic, so that we are justified in calling them a system of natural logic—a term that seems to me preferable to the term common sense, often used for the same thing.

According to natural logic, the fact that every person has talked fluently since infancy makes every man his own authority on the process by which he formulates and communicates. He has merely to consult a common substratum of logic or reason which he and everyone else are supposed to possess. Natural logic says that talking is merely an incidental process concerned strictly with communication, not with formulation of ideas. Talking, or the use of language, is supposed only to 'express' what is essentially already formulated nonlinguistically. Formulation is an independent process, called thought or thinking, and is supposed to be largely indifferent to the nature of particular languages. Languages have grammars, which are assumed to be merely norms of conventional and social correctness, but the use of language is supposed to be guided not so much by them as by correct, rational or intelligent *thinking*.

Thought, in this view, does not depend on grammar but on laws of logic or reason which are supposed to be the same for all observers of the universe—to represent a rationale in the universe that can be 'found' independently by all intelligent observers, whether they speak Chinese or Choctaw. In our own culture, the formulations of mathematics and of formal logic have acquired the reputation of dealing with this order of things: i.e., with the realm and laws of pure thought. Natural logic holds that different languages are essentially parallel methods for expressing this one-and-the-same rationale of thought and, hence, differ really in but minor ways which may seem important only because they are seen at close range. It holds that mathematics, symbolic logic, philosophy, and so on are systems contrasted with language which deal directly with this realm of thought, not that they are themselves specialized extensions of language. The attitude of natural logic is well shown in an old quip about a German grammarian who devoted his whole life to the study of the dative case. From the point of view of natural logic, the dative case and grammar in general are an extremely minor issue. A different attitude is said to have been held by the ancient Arabians: Two princes, so the story goes, quarreled over the honor of putting on the shoes of the most learned grammarian of the realm; whereupon their father, the caliph, is said to have remarked that it was the glory of his kingdom that great grammarians were honored even above kings.

The familiar saying that the exception proves the rule contains a good deal of wisdom, though from the standpoint of formal logic it became an absurdity as soon as 'prove' no longer meant 'put on trial'. The old saw began to be profound psychology from the time it ceased to have standing in logic. What it might well suggest to us today is that, if a rule has absolutely no exceptions, it is not recognized as a rule or as anything else; it is then part of the background of experience of which we tend to remain unconscious. Never having experienced anything in contrast to it, we cannot isolate it and formulate it as a rule until we so enlarge our experience and expand our base of reference that we encounter an interruption of its regularity. The situation is somewhat analogous to that of not missing the water till the well runs dry, or not realizing that we need air till we are choking.

For instance, if a race of people had the physiological defect of being able to see only the color blue, they would hardly be able to formulate the rule that they saw only blue. The term blue would convey no meaning to them, their language would lack color terms, and their words denoting their various sensations of blue would answer to, and translate, our words 'light, dark, white, black,' and so on, not our word 'blue'. In order to formulate the rule or norm of seeing only blue, they would need exceptional moments in which they saw other colors. The phenomenon of gravitation forms a rule without exceptions; needless to say, the untutored person is utterly unaware of any law of gravitation, for it would never enter his head to conceive of a universe in which bodies behaved otherwise than they do at the earth's surface. Like the color blue with our hypothetical race, the law of gravitation is a part of the untutored individual's background, not something he isolates from that background. The law could not be formulated until bodies that always fell were seen in terms of a wider astronomical world in which bodies moved in orbits or went this way and that.

Similarly, whenever we turn our heads, the image of the scene passes across our retinas exactly as it would if the scene turned around us. But this effect is background, and we do not recognize it; we do not see a room turn around us but are conscious only of having turned our heads in a stationary room. If we observe critically while turning the head or eyes quickly, we shall see, no motion it is true, yet a blurring of the scene between two clear views. Normally we are quite unconscious of this continual blurring but seem to be looking about in an unblurred world. Whenever we walk past a tree or house, its image on the retina changes just as if the tree or house were turning on an axis; yet we do not see trees or houses turn as we travel about at ordinary speeds. Sometimes ill-fitting glasses will reveal queer movements in the scene as we look about, but normally we do not see the relative motion of the environment when we move; our psychic make-up is somehow adjusted to disregard whole realms of phenomena that are so all-pervasive as to be irrelevant to our daily lives and needs.

Natural logic contains two fallacies: First, it does not see that the phenomena of a language are to its own speakers largely of a background character and so are outside the critical consciousness and control of the speaker who is expounding natural logic. Hence, when anyone, as a natural logician, is talking about reason, logic, and the laws of correct thinking, he is apt to be simply marching in step with purely grammatical facts that have somewhat of a background character in his own language or family of languages but are by no means universal in all languages and in no sense a common substratum of reason. Second, natural logic confuses agreement about subject matter, attained through use of language, with knowledge of the linguistic process by which agreement is attained: i.e., with the province of the despised (and to its notion superfluous) grammarian. Two fluent speakers, of English let us say, quickly reach a point of assent about the subject matter of their speech; they agree about what their language refers to. One of them, A, can give directions that will be carried out by the other, B, to A's complete satisfaction. Because they thus understand each other so perfectly, A and B, as natural logicians, suppose they must of course know how it is all done. They think, e.g., that it is simply a matter of choosing words to express thoughts. If you ask A to explain how he got B's agreement so readily, he will simply repeat to you, with more or less elaboration or abbreviation, what he said to B. He has no notion of the process involved. The amazingly complex system of linguistic patterns and classifications, which A and B must have in common before they can adjust to each other at all, is all background to A and B.

These background phenomena are the province of the grammarian—or of the linguist, to give him his more modern name as a scientist. The word linguist in common, and especially newspaper, parlance means something entirely different, namely, a person who can quickly attain agreement about subject matter with different people speaking a number of different languages. Such a person is better termed a polyglot or a multilingual. Scientific linguists have long understood that ability to speak a language fluently does not necessarily confer a linguistic knowledge of it, i.e., understanding of its background phenomena and its systematic processes and structure, any more than ability to play a good game of billiards confers or requires any knowledge of the laws of mechanics that operate upon the billiard table.

The situation here is not unlike that in any other field of science. All real scientists have their eyes primarily on background phenomena that cut very little ice, as such, in our daily lives; and yet their studies have a way of bringing out a close relation between these unsuspected realms of fact and such decidedly foreground activities as transporting goods, preparing food, treating the sick, or growing potatoes, which in time may become very much modified, simply because of pure scientific investigation in no way concerned with these brute matters themselves. Linguistics presents a quite similar case; the background phenomena with which it deals are involved in all our foreground activities of talking and of reaching agreement, in all reasoning and arguing of cases, in all law, arbitration, conciliation, contracts, treaties, public opinion, weighing of scientific theories, formulation of scientific results. Whenever agreement or assent is arrived at in human affairs, and whether or not mathematics or other specialized symbolisms are made part of the procedure, *this agreement is reached by linguistic processes, or else it is not reached.*

As we have seen, an overt knowledge of the linguistic processes by which agreement is attained is not necessary to reaching some sort of agreement, but it is certainly no bar thereto; the more complicated and difficult the matter, the more such knowledge is a distinct aid, till the point may be reached—I suspect the modern world has about arrived at it—when the knowledge becomes not only an aid but a necessity. The situation may be likened to that of navigation. Every boat that sails is in the lap of planetary forces; yet a boy can pilot his small craft around a harbor without benefit of geography, astronomy, mathematics, or international politics. To the captain of an ocean liner, however, some knowledge of all these subjects is essential.

When linguists became able to examine critically and scientifically a large number of languages of widely different patterns, their base of reference was expanded; they experienced an interruption of phenomena hitherto held universal, and a whole new order of significances came into their ken. It was found that the background linguistic system (in other words, the grammar) of each language is not merely a reproducing instrument for voicing ideas but rather is itself the shaper of ideas, the program and guide for the individual's mental activity, for his analysis of impressions, for his synthesis of his mental stock in trade. Formulation of ideas is not an independent process, strictly rational in the old sense, but is part of a particular grammar, and differs, from slightly to greatly, between different grammars. We dissect nature along lines laid down by our native languages. The categories and types that we isolate from the world of phenomena we do not find there because they stare every observer in the face; on the contrary, the world is presented in a kaleidoscopic flux of impressions which has to be organized by our minds—and this means largely by the linguistic systems in our minds. We cut nature up, organize it into concepts, and ascribe significances as we do, largely because we are parties to an agreement to organize it in this way—an agreement that holds throughout our speech community and is codified in the patterns of our language. The agreement is, of course, an implicit and unstated one, *but its terms are absolutely obligatory;* we cannot talk at all except by subscribing to the organization and classification of data which the agreement decrees.

This fact is very significant for modern science, for it means that no individual is free to describe nature with absolute impartiality but is constrained to certain modes of interpretation even while he thinks himself most free. The person most nearly free in such respects would be a linguist familiar with very many widely different linguistic systems. As yet no linguist is in any such position. We are thus introduced to a new principle of relativity, which holds that all observers are not led by the same physical evidence to the same picture of the universe, unless their linguistic backgrounds are similar, or can in some way be calibrated.

This rather startling conclusion is not so apparent if we compare only our modern European languages, with perhaps Latin and Greek thrown in for good measure. Among these tongues there is a unanimity of major pattern which at first seems to bear out natural logic. But this unanimity exists only because these tongues are all Indo-European dialects cut to the same basic plan, being historically transmitted from what was long ago one speech community; because the modern dialects have long shared in building up a common culture; and because much of this culture, on the more intellectual side, is derived from the linguistic backgrounds of Latin and Greek. Thus this group of languages satisfies the special case of the clause beginning 'unless' in the statement of the linguistic relativity principle at the end of the preceding paragraph. From this condition follows the unanimity of description of the world in the community of modern scientists. But it must be emphasized that 'all modern Indo-European-speaking observers' is not the same thing as 'all observers'. That modern Chinese or Turkish scientists describe the world in the same terms as Western scientists means, of course only that they have taken over bodily the entire Western system of rationalizations, not that they have corroborated that system from their native posts of observation.

When Semitic, Chinese, Tibetan, or African languages are contrasted with our own, the divergence in analysis of the world becomes more apparent; and, when we bring in the native languages of the Americas, where speech communities for many millenniums have gone their ways independently of each other and of the Old World, the fact that languages dissect nature in many different ways becomes patent. The relativity of all conceptual systems, ours included, and their dependence upon language stand revealed. That American Indians speaking only their native tongues are never called upon to act as scientific observers is in no wise to the point. To exclude the evidence which their languages offer as to what the human mind can do is like expecting botanists to study nothing but food plants and hothouse roses and then tell us what the plant world is like!

Let us consider a few examples. In English we divide most of our words into two classes, which have different grammatical and logical properties. Class 1 we call nouns, e.g., 'house, man', class 2, verbs, e.g., 'hit, run.' Many words of one class can act secondarily as of the other class, e.g., 'a hit, a run', or 'to man (the boat),' but, on the primary level, the division between the classes is absolute. Our language thus gives us a bipolar division of nature. But nature herself is not thus polarized. If it be said that 'strike, turn, run,' are verbs because they denote temporary or short lasting events, i.e., actions, why then is 'fist' a noun? It also is a temporary event. Why are 'lightning, spark, wave, eddy, pulsation, flame, storm, phase, cycle, spasm, noise, emotion' nouns? They are temporary events. If 'man' and 'house' are nouns because they are long-lasting and stable events, i.e., things, what then are 'keep, adhere, extend, project, continue, persist, grow, dwell,' and so on doing among the verbs? If it be objected that 'possess, adhere' are verbs because they are stable relationships rather than stable percepts, why then should 'equilibrium, pressure, current, peace, group, nation, society, tribe, sister,' or any kinship term be among the nouns? It will be found that an 'event' to us means 'what our language classes as a verb' or something analogized therefrom. And it will be found that it is not possible to define 'event, thing, object, relationship,' and so on, from nature, but that to define them always involves a circuitous return to the

Figure [A]
Contrast between a 'temporal' language (English) and a 'timeless' language (Hopi). What are to English differences of time are to Hopi differences in the kind of validity

OBJECTIVE FIELD	SPEAKER (SENDER)	HEARER (RECEIVER)	HANDLING OF TOPIC, RUNNING OF THIRD PERSON
SITUATION 1a.			ENGLISH... "HE IS RUNNING" HOPI... "WARI" (RUNNING. STATEMENT OF FACT)
SITUATION 1b. OBJECTIVE FIELD BLANK DEVOID OF RUNNING			ENGLISH... "HE RAN" HOPI... "WARI" (RUNNING, STATEMENT OF FACT)
SITUATION 2			ENGLISH... "HE IS RUNNING" HOPI... "WARI" (RUNNING, STATEMENT OF FACT)
SITUATION 3 OBJECTIVE FIELD BLANK			ENGLISH... "HE RAN" HOPI... "ERA WARI" (RUNNING. STATEMENT OF FACT FROM MEMORY)
SITUATION 4 OBJECTIVE FIELD BLANK			ENGLISH... "HE WILL RUN" HOPI... "WARIKNI" (RUNNING, STATEMENT OF EXPECTATION)
SITUATION 5 OBJECTIVE FIELD BLANK			ENGLISH... "HE RUNS" (E.G. ON THE TRACK TEAM) HOPI... "WARIKNGWE" (RUNNING. STATEMENT OF LAW)

grammatical categories of the definer's language.

In the Hopi language, 'lightning, wave, flame, meteor, puff of smoke, pulsation' are verbs—events of necessarily brief duration cannot be anything but verbs. 'Cloud' and 'storm' are at about the lower limit of duration for nouns. Hopi, you see, actually has a classification of events (or linguistic isolates) by duration type, something strange to our modes of thought. On the other hand, in Nootka, a language of Vancouver Island, all words seem to us to be verbs, but really there are no classes 1 and 2; we have, as it were, a monistic view of nature that gives us only one class of word for all kinds of events. 'A house occurs' or 'it houses' is the way of saying 'house', exactly like 'a flame occurs' or 'it burns'. These terms seem to us like verbs because they are inflected for durational and temporal nuances, so that the suffixes of the word for house event make it mean long-lasting house, temporary house, future house, house that used to be, what started out to be a house, and so on.

Hopi has one noun that covers every thing or being that flies, with the exception of birds, which class is denoted by another noun. The former noun may be said to denote the class (*FC–B*)—flying class minus bird. The Hopi actually call insect, airplane, and aviator all by the same word, and feel no difficulty about it. The situation, of course, decides any possible confusion among very disparate members of a broad linguistic class, such as this class (*FC–B*). This class seems to us too large and inclusive, but so would our word 'snow' to an Eskimo. We have the same word for falling snow, snow on the ground, snow packed hard like ice, slushy snow, wind/driven flying snow—whatever the situation may be. To an Eskimo, this all-inclusive word would be almost unthinkable; he would say that falling snow, slushy snow, and so on, are sensuously and operationally different, different things to contend with; he uses different words for them and for other kinds of snow. The Aztecs go even farther than we in the opposite direction, with 'cold', 'ice', and 'snow' all represented by the same basic word with different terminations; 'ice' is the noun form; 'cold,' the adjectival form; and for 'snow,' 'ice-mist'.

What surprises most is to find that various grand generalizations of the Western world, such as time, velocity, and matter, are not essential to the construction of a consistent picture of the universe. The psychic experiences that we class under these headings are, of course, not destroyed; rather, categories derived from other kinds of experiences take over the rulership of the cosmology and seem to function just as well. Hopi may be called a timeless language. It recognises psychological time, which is much like Bergson's 'duration,' but this 'time' is quite unlike the mathematical time, T, used by our physicists. Among the peculiar properties of Hopi time are that it varies with each observer, does not permit of simultaneity, and has zero dimensions; i.e., it cannot be given a number greater than one. The Hopi do not say, 'I stayed five days,' but 'I left on the fifth day'. A word referring to this kind of time, like the word day, can have no plural. The puzzle picture (Figure A) will give mental exercise to anyone who would like to figure out how the Hopi verb gets along without tenses. Actually, the only practical use of our tenses, in one-verb sentences, is to distinguish among five typical situations, which are symbolized in the picture. The timeless Hopi verb does not distinguish between the present, past, and future of the event itself but must always indicate what type of validity the *speaker* intends the statement to have: (a) report of an event (situations 1, 2, 3, in the picture); (b) expectation of an event (situation 4); (c) generalization or law about events (situation 5). Situation 1, where the speaker and listener are in contact with the same objective field, is divided by our language into the two conditions 1*a* and 1*b*, which it calls present and past, respectively. This division is unnecessary for a language which assures one that the statement is a report.

Hopi grammar, by means of its forms called aspects and modes, also makes it easy to distinguish among momentary, continued, and repeated occurrences, and to indicate the actual sequence of reported events. Thus the universe can be described without recourse to a concept of dimensional time. How would a physics constructed along these lines work, with no T (time) in its equations? Perfectly, as far as I can see, though of course it would require different ideology and perhaps different mathematics. Of course V (velocity) would have to go too. The Hopi language has no word really equivalent to our 'speed' or 'rapid'. What translates these terms is usually a word meaning intense or very, accompanying any verb of motion. Here is a clue to the nature of our new physics. We may have to introduce a new term I, intensity. Every thing and event will have an I, whether we regard the thing or event as moving or as just enduring or being. Perhaps the I of an electric charge will turn out to be its voltage, or potential. We shall use clocks to measure some intensities, or, rather, some *relative* intensities, for the absolute intensity of anything will be meaningless. Our old friend acceleration will still be there but doubtless under a new name. We shall perhaps call it V, meaning not velocity but variation. Perhaps all growths and accumulations will be regarded as V's. We should not have the concept of rate in the temporal sense, since, like velocity, rate introduces a mathematical and linguistic time. Of course we know that all measurements are ratios, but the measurements of intensities made by comparison with the standard intensity of a clock or a planet we do not treat as ratios, any more than we so treat a distance made by comparison with a yardstick.

A scientist from another culture that used time and velocity would have great difficulty in getting us to understand these concepts. We should talk about the intensity of a chemical reaction; he would speak of its velocity or its rate, which words we should at first think were simply words for intensity in his language. Likewise, he at first would think that intensity was simply our own word for velocity. At first we should agree, later we should begin to disagree, and it might dawn upon both sides that different systems of rationalization were being used. He would find it very hard to make us understand what he really meant by velocity of a chemical reaction. We should have no words that would fit. He would try to explain it by likening it to a running horse, to the difference between a good horse and a lazy horse. We should try to show him, with a superior laugh that his analogy also was a matter of different intensities, aside from which there was little similarity between a horse and a chemical reaction in a beaker. We should point out that a running horse is moving relative to the ground, whereas the material in the beaker is at rest.

One significant contribution to science from the linguistic point of view may be the greater development of our sense of perspective. We shall no longer be able to see a few recent dialects of the Indo-European family, and the rationalizing techniques elaborated from their patterns, as the apex of the evolution of the human mind, nor their present wide spread as due to any survival from fitness or to anything but a few events of history—events that could be called fortunate only from the parochial point of view of the favored parties. They, and our own thought processes with them, can no longer be envisioned as spanning the gamut of reason and knowledge but only as one constellation in a galactic expanse. A fair realization of the incredible degree of diversity of linguistic system that ranges over the globe leaves one with an inescapable feeling that the human spirit is inconceivably old; that the few thousand years of history covered by our written records are no more than the thickness of a pencil mark on the scale that measures our past experience on this planet; that the events of these recent millenniums spell nothing in any evolutionary wise, that the race has taken no sudden spurt, achieved no commanding synthesis during recent millenniums, but has only played a little with a few of the linguistic formulations and views of nature bequeathed from an inexpressibly longer past. Yet neither this feeling nor the sense of precarious dependence of all we know upon linguistic tools which themselves are largely unknown need be discouraging to science but should, rather, foster that humility which accompanies the true scientific spirit, and thus forbid that arrogance of the mind which hinders real scientific curiosity and detachment.

4.4   Research based on the Whorfian hypothesis is thus directed towards differences between languages rather than similarities. It is concerned, not with verbal habits deriving from the mere fact of language acquisition, but rather with those habits deriving from some characteristic aspect of one or more languages, and how such habits affect cognition. To put it another way: what aspects of, for example, the English language, give it its unique 'Englishness', and how does this 'Englishness' affect cognition differently from, say, the 'Navahoness' of Navaho?

lexicon

4.5   Whorf was particularly interested in the differences between English and American Indian languages, and delighted in cataloguing differences in lexicon, or stock of words, for describing common areas of experience (cf. the snow and flying examples in Whorf's article). He also looked for grammatical differences, suggesting, for example, that the absence of noun-verb distinctions in Nootka is related to 'a monistic view of nature'. Similarly he regarded Hopi verbs, which distinguish the duration and certainty of events rather than when they occurred, as congruent with a world view that is timeless and ahistorical.

4.6   But although Whorf did more than the early ethnolinguists to make explicit links between differences in language and in the way in which the external world is analysed, his arguments are unfortunately tautological: the characteristics of a language which are said to have brought about a particular world-view are the only evidence advanced in support of this world-view. (For example, the Nootka do not distinguish between nouns and verbs—therefore they have a monistic view of nature—but how do we know this?—because they don't distinguish between nouns and verbs.)

4.7   The Whorfian hypothesis would obviously gain in plausibility if it could be shown that particular language characteristics influenced individual behaviour on cognitive tasks such as recognition, classification, or problem-solving—and this has therefore been the strategy of more recent researchers.

4.8   At the grammatical level, a major study is Carroll and Casagrande's 'Experiment II' (1958) on object classification in English and Navaho (American Indian) children. Navaho-speaking children learn at a very early age that verbs of handling (drop, hold, etc.) require different verb stems according to the shape, or form, of the object being handled. Therefore Carroll and Casagrande predicted that Navaho-speaking children would classify objects primarily on the basis of form. In contrast to this, the English language provides no such pressure towards form-discrimination.

4.9   Subjects for the Carroll and Casagrande study were three groups of children aged 3–10 years: white middle-class children from Boston, USA, dominantly Navaho-speaking and dominantly English-speaking Navahos. Each child was shown a pair of objects which differed from each other in two respects (e.g. yellow rope, blue stick). Then a third object, similar to each of the first two in one respect, was presented (e.g. blue rope) and the child was asked to choose which of the first two objects went best with the third item. Ten such sets of objects were used, employing combinations of size, colour, shape and Navaho verb-stem.

4.10 The Whorfian hypothesis received support insofar that, at every age, Navaho-dominant children made significantly more choices on the basis of form than the English-dominant Navaho, who classified primarily by colour. However, from the age of five, the Boston children proved to be even more 'Navaho' in their choices than the Navaho-dominants! Carroll and Casagrande attributed this somewhat embarrassing finding to the fairly recent increase in popularity of formboard toys designed to encourage children to sort by shape, particularly among the middle-classes[1]. They amended their hypothesis to read: 'the tendency of a child to match objects on the basis of form . . . may be enhanced by either of two kinds of experiences; (a) learning to speak a language, like Navaho . . . or (b) practice with toys and other objects involving the fitting of forms and shapes . . .'

lexical level

4.11 At the lexical level, an extreme version of the Whorfian hypothesis would assert that if a language lacks a word for something, that 'thing' cannot be recognized or classified. So far there is no evidence that this is so; rather, the evidence supports a weaker version of the hypothesis, *viz.* that lexical differences influence other cognitive processes only insofar as they help or hinder speakers of the language concerned to be aware of certain aspects of their environment and communicate easily about them. One example of evidence supporting this weaker version of the Whorfian hypothesis is Berry's finding (3.17) that the level of visual-spatial skill correlated positively with the number of geo-spatial distinctions made in a language. Similarly, as part of a wide-ranging study of the cultural factors that need to be taken into account in order to teach Western-style mathematics effectively to Liberian Kpelle schoolchildren, Gay and Cole (1967; further reading) have shown how differences in Kpelle and American ways of expressing logical connections give rise to different strengths and weaknesses in solving formal logic problems.

codability

4.12 Such differences in awareness and ease of communication are referred to as contrasts in *codability*, a term devised by Brown and Lenneberg (1958). Following on from Zipf, who showed that in many languages the longer the word, the less frequently it is used, Brown and Lenneberg defined as highly codable those categories which can be named *quickly* and *consistently*, with a *frequently-used*, usually *short, single* word.

Activity 5
Codability
Allow about ten minutes

Q1 Give some examples of English words which have become shortened as their frequency of occurrence has increased.

Q2 Father, second cousin, aunt, brother, great-great-grandfather, are examples of English kinship categories. Which are highly codable, and which have a low codability? In our culture, what attitudes to kin do these differences in codability reflect?

Q3 Why are translations of books almost always considered inferior to the originals?

Q4 Why is there a need for technical dictionaries, glossaries to these blocks, ILEA's guide to educational terms 'In Other Words', etc?

---

[1] *Casagrande found in 1960 that a group of Harlem school-children, 'less educationally advanced' than the Boston group, were very close in performance to the English-dominant Navahos.*

Discussion of Activity 5

Q1   Plane; phone; pop; car (from motorized carriage); etc; also abbreviations—TV; LP; AA; etc.

Q2   Father, aunt, brother—high codability; second cousin, great-great-grandfather—low codability. Unlike some so-called 'primitive' cultures, we tend to consider kin nearest to us in time, and 'blood' more important than ancestors or extended family.

Q3   Different languages rarely employ exactly equivalent terms. This often leads to a clumsiness of style and the feeling that shades of meaning have been lost in translation.

Q4   Almost inevitably specialists develop many highly codable terms to communicate briefly and precisely with other specialists in their field about the things which concern them. Such terms often confound the layman or learner who (if they do so at all) are likely to have longer, less precise and less 'generally-agreed' ways of describing the same phenomena.

4.13   Brown and Lenneberg (1958) investigated the relationship between codability and memory, using a colour recognition task. The colour spectrum is particularly useful in the study of codability because it is a real continuum i.e. no natural 'objective' breaks occur, and it is therefore a matter of cultural consensus as to how it is divided. Using two groups of English-speaking students, Brown and Lenneberg obtained from the first group codability scores for twenty-four colours, based on (a) speed of naming—the average time subjects took to think of a name for each colour; (b) length—the number of syllables used; and (c) consistency of naming—the degree of agreement between subjects and 'within' each subject on two occasions. Subjects in the second group were shown four of the twenty-four colours and then, after delays varying between seven seconds and three minutes, were shown the same four colours again in an array of 120, and asked to point them out. Brown and Lenneberg hypothesized that the lower the codability of a colour, the less likely it was to be remembered and recognized correctly; and that as the length of delay increased, memory 'storage' would become more difficult and hence codability more important. Their results confirmed these hypotheses, giving rise to correlations between codability scores and subjects' performance on the recognition task of 0.43 at seven seconds up to 0.52 at three minutes (both $p = <0.05$).

4.14   Brown and Lenneberg also report a similar study using Zuni Indian as well as English subjects. The Zuni language codes with a single term the colours we distinguish as orange and yellow. As predicted, Zuni speakers confused the two in the recognition task far more frequently than English subjects, while the performance of bi-lingual Zunis fell in-between. However, Lenneberg has since noted that these results seem specific to the colour array they used; other arrays have given very different results. Lantz and Stefflre (1964) devised a different measure of codability—communication accuracy—which is based on a view of memory as communication with oneself over time. They argue that communication with others is a good approximation to the memory process, and their measure of communication accuracy is based on asking subjects to 'describe this item in such a way that another person will be able to pick it out'. Lantz and Stefflre show that their measure of codability is a better predictor of memory for colours than Brown and Lenneberg's because their codability-recognition correlations were higher and consistent on two very different colour arrays. However, the whole field is still one in which there is much disagreement, and much still to find out[1].

[1]See Bruner (1974), Chapter 2, for further reading in this area.

Summary

4.15   The hypothesis that speakers of markedly different languages will consequently hold different world-views is intuitively attractive but difficult to test.
The evidence we have suggests that, in fact, the differences between cultures
in this respect are a matter of degree rather than kind. Lexical and grammatical differences may facilitate or hinder certain discriminations and kinds of
problem-solving, but seem unlikely to prevent them; cognitive processes and
types of thinking are almost certainly less culture-specific than are language
differences. Moreover, (cf. Carroll and Casagrande) other cultural factors
may overrule any influence which language differences may have on cognitive
processes. Finally, there is the evolutionary question of causation—whether,
as Whorf implies, language has always determined the concepts and
categories used in thought, or whether (the anti-Whorf view) language simply
reflects the concepts and categories which have evolved in the course of a
culture's adaptation to its ecology. One possible resolution is afforded by
Berry's type of model, in which the *interaction* between ecology, language and
individual thought is stressed.

4.16   We shall return to the subject of language differences in Part 2, where some of
the implications of sub-cultural variations in language forms and usage will
be explored.

5 Cognitive development: a Piagetian view

5.1   In Blocks 4 and 6, Piagetian and more conventional psychometric concepts of
intelligence were discussed. The distinction between these concepts is also
applicable to this and the next section, so it may be helpful to summarize
briefly the differences between the two approaches—while stressing that their
contributions arc complementary rather than mutually exclusive. The
psychometric approach depends largely on statistical analysis; it is concerned
with the structure of intellectual skills and the 'end-product' of individual
differences in scores on tests designed to quantify cognitive development. The
Piagetian approach has its theoretical roots in logic and mathematical theory,
and is more concerned with the qualitative nature of the content and sequence
of development, and the degree to which this is universal. The Piagetian
testing situation is thus more flexible (the 'clinical method'), to allow exploration of the reasoning behind responses.

Piagetian stages

5.2   In all Western cultures the content and sequence of development appears to
be qualitatively the same, although the *rate* of that development—the age at
which Piagetian stages are attained—may differ. (For example, lower socio-
economic status tends to be associated with slower progression through the
stages.) However, Western cultures are relatively homogeneous—certainly
too much so to confirm any universal theory about cognitive development.
Since the late 1950s therefore, an increasing amount of research has been
carried out in cultures which differ radically from our own.

5.3   Unfortunately such studies have mostly used different combinations of cultures and tasks relating to only one of the Piagetian stages, making an overall
assessment impossible. In particular, no studies exist which encompass the
four global stages, and work on the sensorimotor and formal stages is sparse.
The bulk of research is concentrated on the concrete operational stage, and

conservation

Figure 3
Percentage of subjects
attaining the concrete
operational stage as a
function of age: a
representation of trends
(from Dasen, 1972)

especially on conservation, and therefore we shall be primarily concerned with this.

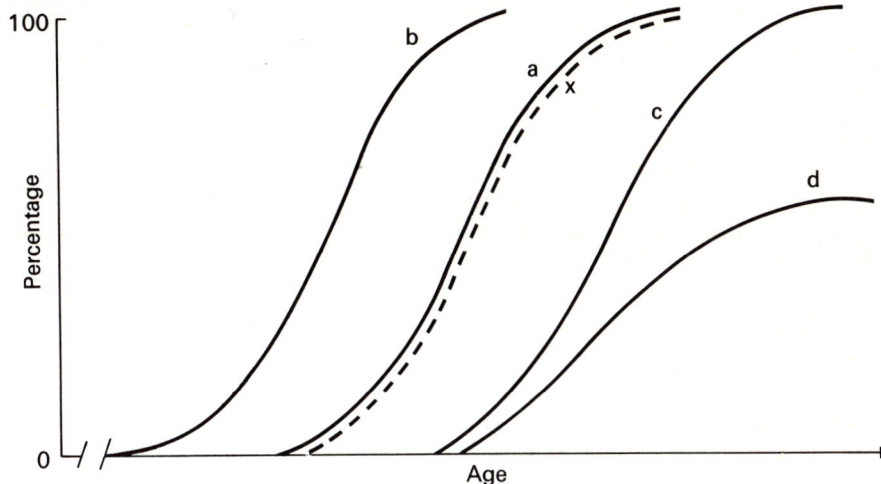

a   The concept develops at the same time as in European children (x).
b   The concept develops earlier, or more quickly.
c   The concept develops later, or more slowly; there is a 'time-lag', or retarded development; all children, however, eventually reaching concrete operational thinking.
d   The concept starts to develop at the same time or later, but the curve is *asymptotic*—it flattens out at the higher ages: some children, and even adults, do not reach the concrete operational stage.

5.4   All cross-cultural studies of concrete operations report that *some* subjects attain this stage; but there are considerable differences in the age and proportion of those who do so. Dasen (1972) has devised a set of curves which represent the four main trends found in cross-cultural research (see Figure 3). Findings of type (a) and (b) are relatively rare; (c) and (d) are much more common, with the time-lag in (c) varying between one to six years.

5.5   Findings of type (a), (b) and (c) highlight the influence of cultural factors on the *rate* of development, but nonetheless they provide support for the universality of structures at the concrete operational stage. Type (d) findings, however, suggest that the concrete operational stage may *not* be universal. Some studies reporting such a curve have been done with children only, leaving open the possibility that if older age groups had been included, the apparent (d) curve would have become a (c) curve. But other studies which have included adults have also shown a (d) curve. Such apparent failure to attain the concrete operational stage raises three basic questions which are posed in the context of Activity 6, and provide the structure for the remainder of this section. You may find it useful to try Activity 6 (p. 46) both before and after reading the remainder of this section—before as a check on your understanding of material in Block 4, and after as a check on what you have read in this section.

Factors in the test situation

5.6   Various research studies have suggested that results may be affected by one or more of the following: the nature of the dialogue between experimenter and child; the fact that it is normally the *experimenter* who manipulates the material; and the type of material used. In several cases these points have been demonstrated by changing the procedures and/or materials, and showing that the responses of the children differ accordingly.

5.7   Not surprisingly, the heavy verbal emphasis in Piagetian research has given rise to a number of problems in the cross-cultural context. The most obvious are those which arise from translation, but with care these can be overcome. Other problems more peculiar to the Piagetian interview may arise in connection with the pattern of verbal interaction that is required. The experimenter

Activity 6	Failure to attain the concrete operational stage	20 minutes (2 × 10)
	Before reading on	After reading Section 5
Q1 In the Piagetian interview, the child is asked to comment on the experimenter's manipulation of materials, while the experimenter explores his reasoning by encouraging him to present arguments in support of his judgements. **a** What factors in the cross-cultural test situation might be responsible for apparent failure to attain the concrete operational stage? **b** How could you find out whether they were responsible?		
Q2 Above all, Piaget's theory stresses the adaptive nature of behaviour. What cultural differences, compared with Western cultures, might be associated with 'late' occurrence or non-occurrence of concrete operations?		
Q3 Piaget's stages may be considered as points on a yardstick of cognitive development. If fewer stages appear to be achieved by fewer people in non-Western cultures, what could this imply about them, and about Piaget's theory?		

may only have a very limited knowledge of the subject's language, restricting his ability to follow up his questioning. On the other hand, the child may not be used to expressing and maintaining an opinion while being questioned. For example, Dasen (1974) was unable to use the normal procedure of suggestion and counter-suggestion to test the stability of Aborigine children's responses because the children took counter-suggestions as criticism and changed their answers; it was impossible to tell whether they had changed their minds, or were simply giving answers that they knew to be wrong but thought would please the European 'authority figure'. Similarly, Greenfield (1966) found that unschooled Senegalese children would not respond to the obvious opinion-seeking question, 'why do you *think* or *say* X is true?' whereas they would respond to the simple 'why is X true?'

5.8   One way of avoiding such problems is to require the child to do some, or all, of the manipulation of materials as a non-verbal means to investigate reasoning. This technique was used by Bovet (1973) in her study of unschooled Algerian children. Bovet found that, while the conservation of length followed the Genevan pattern of gradual development[1] and simply appeared at a slightly older age (10–12 years instead of 9), conservation of quantity and weight both showed an unusual pattern: children of 7–8 years of age, and those over 12, were making conservation judgements, but children of 9–11 were not. Bovet suspected that the 7–8 year olds might be 'pseudo-conservers', particularly since she was unable to obtain verbal justifications for their judgements, even after drawing their attention to the changes in dimensions. To see if she was right to doubt their understanding of

[1]*Piaget, working in Geneva, has identified for each particular concept, such as conservation, a number of sub-stages through which the child develops over time, culminating in responses which show logical support for judgements.*

invariance, Bovet gave them tests which required manipulation rather than words, e.g. to pour equal amounts of water into glasses differing in height, diameter, or both, or to indicate the level to which the same amount of water would rise if it were to be poured into glasses of different dimensions. In the Genevan pattern, these problems are solved about the same time as the usual conservation ones, but in this case the 7–8 year olds responded incorrectly. When Bovet gave them the original tests again, she found that they had changed from their initial conserving responses to non-conservation judgements based on specific dimensions.

5.9   Manipulation of materials by the child rather than the experimenter may, in some circumstances, actually change the child's pattern of reasoning. Greenfield (1966) found in her study of liquid conservation among Wolof children in Senegal that when *she* poured the liquid, many of her rural unschooled subjects and urban first grade entrants gave non-conservation responses such as, 'there's more in this glass because you poured it'; the children used her actions to rationalize the perceptual discrepancy between initial equality and later apparent inequality. Greenfield called this 'action-magic' thinking—the attribution of 'magical' powers to an authority figure such as the experimenter. But she found that when another group of rural unschooled children did the pouring *themselves*, the proportion of conservers more than doubled, and 'action-magic' reasons disappeared.

5.10 To check on the reason for this dramatic change, Greenfield extended her previous research with schooled children. Having already found that children with only seven months or so of schooling showed no signs of 'magical' thinking in the experimenter-pouring condition, she now gave the self-pouring task to a similar group of school-children. They proved no better conservers than the first schooled group, indicating that the 'power' of the child-pouring technique did not stem from the simple fact of activity. Greenfield therefore concluded that this technique undermines the unschooled child's magical mode of thought. He does not attribute special powers of thought to himself, and he is bound to have more accurate cause-and-effect notions with regard to his own actions than to others; without the distraction of adult intervention, he is, to paraphrase Greenfield, 'free to solve the problem rather than the experimenter'.

5.11 In both the studies of conservation cited above, the material used was water. The impact of different stimulus materials in different cultures has not yet been fully or systematically assessed, but a number of studies suggest that the occurrence of conservation responses may in part be dependent on the material used—for example, fruit cordial, sugar, earth, water and plasticine have all been used in continuous quantity experiments, sometimes with differing results (Lloyd, 1972).

Cultural factors in the development of concrete operations

5.12 Certain cultural differences may thus give rise to 'wrong' assessments of the stage a child has reached. Nevertheless there are several studies, again mostly of conservation, which suggest that cultural differences may really affect the development of concrete operations. In particular, the effects of differences in daily activities and the more general variables of schooling and contact with Western cultures have been investigated.

5.13 Besides her research with Algerian children, Bovet also investigated the relationship between conservation and life-style in illiterate adults aged 35–50 years, who were either rural village-dwellers or rural migrants to Algiers. The village men were mainly involved in agriculture, and the urban men in selling goods around the city; both groups had to walk some distance to work. In contrast the women were almost totally house-bound. For neither sex was there any pressure to accomplish any activity within a specific time limit. Bovet hypothesized that the concrete operational stage would be more likely to be achieved with those concepts used frequently in regular daily activities—in this case, quantity, weight and possibly length, but not speed or time.

5.14 In general this proved to be the case. Conservation of liquid quantity presented no difficulties, while problems dealing with speed and time were only rarely solved correctly. Interesting differences between men and women's responses occurred in the conservation of length and weight. For length, all the men immediately gave conservation responses, whereas the women only reached them by trial-and-error—a difference Bovet attributes, perhaps simplistically, to the fact that only the men were used to travelling distances, choosing short cuts, etc. For weight, the men gave either stable conservation responses or truly non-conserving ones, whereas two unusual responses were made by some of the women, as Bovet describes (1973, pp. 324–5):

a Several female subjects refused to make a judgement after one of the clay balls had been broken into several pieces. These subjects said that it was impossible for them to judge without first weighing the clay in their hands, and refused to 'guess'.

b Moreover, in several instances, the initial response was a conservation one. Then when the experimenter, in an attempt to obtain a justification for this response, pointed out the differences in appearance of the two objects, the subjects would no longer give a conservation response. In the course of the dialogue, however, the subjects would return to a conservation judgement, and would be able to relate the various dimensions of the objects by means of a reasoning based on compensation. These adults' reactions seem to replicate in a condensed sequence the developmental trends noted in the children where an initial non-operational conservation finally becomes, at a later stage, an explicit conservation judgement.

For some of the nonconserving subjects, all that was required for them to grasp the notion of conservation was to weigh the two pieces of clay once on a pair of scales in front of them. They then accompanied their judgements by logical justifications and, what is more, generalized their conservation responses to various changes in shape.

It has been noted, however, that in the case of children a single demonstration is not sufficient to elicit a more advanced judgement (Smedslund, 1961). We conclude therefore, that in these adult subjects an underlying logical way of apprehending the problem coexists with an intuitive approach.

5.15 In her study of the Wolof, mentioned earlier in this section, Greenfield (1966) provides an interesting parallel to Bovet's finding that intuitive and logical approaches may lead to the same end. She contrasts the conservation reasons of her Wolof subjects with those given by American children. For both a sense of 'no change' was crucial to conservation, but they appeared to attain this end by different means. American children used reasons based on a sense of conflict between how things appear, and how they 'really are', e.g. 'it looks like more but it is really the same' (Bruner et al. 1966, Chapter 9). Wolof reasons for conservation were based in the past, focusing on the initial equalizing operation, e.g. 'I made them the same' (in the case of the unschooled self-pourers), or, 'this one and this one were equal' (in the case of the schoolchildren for whom Greenfield poured). The appearance–reality schema of the American child was never used by the Wolof children; Greenfield found this distinction very difficult to express in the Wolof language and, when she used it, the children appeared not to understand it.

schema

Reading
Cultural variations in
cognitive skills
Goodnow (1970)
Reader 2, p. 97

5.16 Returning to the theme of links between conservation and cultural differences in daily activities, you should now read the article by J. J. Goodnow (1970) 'Cultural variations in cognitive skills' (p. 97 in the second volume of the Reader). Goodnow provides some resolution to the problem of single studies by drawing together several overlapping pieces of research. She makes the point that as one moves away from a technological society, tasks do not become uniformly more difficult; hence one should be wary of assuming conservation to be a general skill, and should rather seek out the differences between cultures on various tasks and attempt to match these to specific differences in experience. Goodnow suggests that a major difference between cultures lies in visualizing or 'imaging' skills—the ability to transform material in the head. The source of such skills might be two-fold: an attitude of readiness to stop and think ahead, and the tools to be able to do so—for which experiences in physical and mental 'shuffling' are necessary.

imaging skills

5.17 Turning now to the influence of more general cultural variables on the development of concrete operations, an obvious one is extent and type of schooling. But the evidence conflicts as to its importance. For example, Greenfield (1966) found that, by the age of 11–13 years, all her schooled Wolof subjects had attained conservation of quantity in contrast to only 50 per cent of her unschooled sample. On the other hand, Price-Williams (1961) found that, despite their lack of schooling, 100 per cent of his sample of Tiv children in Nigeria has achieved this conservation by the age of eight years. He notes that the children's behaviour during the experiments indicated an active, manipulative approach to the physical world—unlike the Wolof, they would spontaneously perform and reverse the operation themselves. Commenting on these findings, Bruner (1974, p. 46) writes:

> Such self-initiated action . . . may well be the key to the great disparity between the two cultures in spontaneous conservation results.
>
> It may be that a collective, rather than individual, value orientation develops where the individual lacks power over the physical world. Lacking personal power, he has no notion of personal importance. In terms of his cognitive categories, now, he will be less likely to set himself apart from others and the physical world, he will be less self-conscious at the same time that he places less value on himself.[1] Thus, mastery over the physical world and individualistic self-consciousness will appear together in a culture, in contrast to a collective orientation and a realistic view in which people's attitudes and actions are not placed in separate conceptual pigeonholes from physical events.[2]

5.18 Bruner goes on to propose that there may be a developmental basis for these two contrasting value orientations. Drawing on the observations of a French anthropologist, J. Rabain-Zempléni, he suggests broad differences in child-rearing practices and infant experience which may be responsible for the development of these different value orientations. He writes (Bruner, 1974, pp. 47–8):

> Rabain-Zempléni's naturalistic observations confirm the hypothesis derived from the conservation behaviour of the unschooled children, that Wolof children lack manipulatory experience, for she notes that manipulation of objects is an occasional and secondary activity for the child from two to four and that, furthermore, the Wolof child's 'self-image does not have to rest in the same way as in Europe on the power which he has over objects, but rather on that which he has over other bodies'. She also notes that verbal interchanges between children and adults often concern the relations which

---

[1] *(See 5.7 for the Wolof response to questioning about their thoughts.)*
[2] *(See 5.9–5.10 on 'action-magic' thinking among the Wolof as an example of this lack of differentiation between the physical and the social.)*

Kids at carnival

are supposed to exist between people but rarely concern explanations of natural phenomena. At the same time as the Wolof child's manipulation of the physical, inanimate world fails to be encouraged in isolation from social relations, the personal desires and intentions which would isolate him from the group are also discouraged. Thus, a collective orientation does not simply arise as a by-product of individual powerlessness *vis-à-vis* the inanimate world but is systematically encouraged as socialization progresses. Western society recognises individual intention and desire as a positive function of age. According to Rabain-Zempléni, Wolof society does the reverse: the newborn child is treated as a person full of personal desire and intention; after he reaches the age of two, the adults in his milieu increasingly subordinate his desires to the ends of the group; he becomes less and less an individual, more and more a member of a collectivity . . .

Most intriguing is Rabain-Zempléni's observation that in the natural situation of sharing a quantity among several persons, a situation not too different from the second half of the conservation experiment where a quantity is divided among six beakers, more attention is paid to which person receives the substance at what point in the distribution than to the amount received. It is like their conservation explanations: more attention is focused on the person pouring—the social aspect of the situation—than on the purely physical aspect, the amount of water.

5.19   The distinction drawn here by Bruner between collective and individual value orientations will be raised again in Sections 6 (with reference to African concepts of intelligence) and 8 (with reference to sub-cultural differences in language). Meanwhile, we return to the relationship between schooling and the development of concrete operations. If Bruner's 'individual physical mastery' (cf. Goodnow's 'physical shuffling practice') is considered the crucial variable, rather than schooling, then conflicting results might be explained as follows. Where an orientation towards individual physical mastery exists in the culture, as for the Tiv or Chinese, there is no direct relationship between schooling and conservation; but where it is absent, as for the Wolof, then schooling may fill the gap and therefore show a relationship with conservation.[1] In line with this type of argument a number of researchers have attempted to investigate the effect of the—admittedly imprecise—variable of contact with European culture and cognitive values. A particularly interesting study is that by Dasen (1974), for it relates directly to the work of Berry (3.17 ff.).

5.20   Dasen chose to study two groups of Central Australian Aborigines, who were similar in all respects except the length of their contact with Europeans and the extent to which traditional values and activities have persisted in their groups. Both groups live in semi-desert country west of Alice Springs; the group living at the Hermannsburg Mission was rated as medium-contact (0.39 out of a maximum 1.00 on an index of contact made up of seventeen variables, which included language, home and school physical environment, leisure activities, Europeans in population etc.), while the group living at the more recently established Areyonga Government Settlement was rated as low-contact (0.13). In Berry's terms these were respectively 'transitional' and 'traditional' groups. Dasen compared them with a group of European lower-middle-class primary schoolchildren in Canberra.

---

[1]*You should note, however, that schooling* does *appear to be crucial in the development of formal operations. To take an example from the few studies that exist, Goodnow and Bethon (1966) found that, in Hong Kong, combinational tasks—which stand on the borderline between concrete and formal operations—were definitely sensitive to lack of schooling. They suggest that this reflects the unschooled child's greater reliance on perceptual patterns and action models for reasoning than on the 'transformations in the head', which Euro-American education particularly encourages.*

5.21   Following previous studies which showed significant differences in the rate of development of conservation in favour of more Western-like groups, Dasen hypothesized that operational development would be qualitatively the same in his Aborigine and European samples, but that the rate of development would be slower for the Aborigines, especially for the low-contact group. Furthermore, he formed an ecological hypothesis, based on the fact that the environment of Central Australian Aborigines, like that of the Eskimos, demands—at least traditionally—a hunting, travelling, and food-gathering way of life, and highly developed concepts of space. In contrast, concepts of number and measurement are relatively undeveloped because, Dasen suggests, the ecology hardly requires them. Any necessary measurement is done by eye or touch, while numbers above four are indicated by an open hand, or by 'many', 'a big mob'. Individuals are known by their name or tracks, and a hunter only hunts and spears one animal at a time, even though he may see several together. Thus Dasen hypothesized: Aborigines, because of their ecological and cultural background, will develop spatial concepts more readily than 'logico-mathematical' ones (i.e. those related to number and measurement), in contrast to the European children who will follow the Genevan pattern of developing the two types of concept simultaneously, or even logico-mathematical slightly earlier than spatial concepts.

5.22   Dasen used eight Piagetian tasks, five relating to logico-mathematical concepts (conservation of quantity/weight/volume/length, and a seriation task) and three to spatial concepts (orders, rotation, horizontality). He found support for all his hypotheses, thus confirming previous findings that European contact supplies some kind of cognitive 'ambiance' favourable to the development of concrete operations, and providing further support for Berry's ecology-skill model (at least as applied to hunting peoples). In both cases, however, far more detailed analysis is still needed in the definition and matching of experience and abilities.

Summary

norm

5.23   Not all concrete operations, including conservation on which we have focused, are achieved by every member of all non-Western cultures; and those that are achieved generally show a time-lag behind Genevan norms. And, as far as they have been studied, the same is even more true of formal operations. In other words, when measured against the parameters set out by Piaget, other cultures do not achieve 'full' cognitive development. But how far is the yardstick relevant?

5.24   A major 'deficiency' appears to be a lack of contact with, or similarity to, Western value systems and the sort of knowledge and learning behaviour emphasized in Western schools. This suggests that Piagetian theory is rooted within our own culture to a greater extent than we should have realized without cross-cultural research. But to say that to have abilities like ours you need a culture like ours, neither furthers our understanding of cognitive functioning, nor is it strictly true. On the one hand both Bovet and Greenfield have found that different modes of thought can lead to the same results. On the other hand, several investigations have shown that those 'Piagetian' concepts necessary to a certain life-style will develop regardless of Western contact or schooling.

5.25   Interestingly, despite the apparent cultural bias in Piagetian theory, no part of it has so far been definitely refuted by cross-cultural research—although such research has highlighted the need for the theory to be elaborated with reference to cultural influences on the development and difficulty level of concepts. Yet the appropriateness to other cultures of the Piagetian yardstick of development remains debatable; and in the final part of Section 6 we shall look at other cultures' own concepts of intelligence and definitions of 'full' cognitive development. For the moment, you may find it helpful to revise this section by turning back to Activity 6.

6 Cognitive capacity

heredity-environment 6.1
debate
IQ

Part 1 of Block 6 ended with a discussion of the heredity-environment debate, and the accompanying articles by Jensen, Stinchcombe, and Bodmer and Cavalli-Sforza, considered, in some detail, the differences in IQ found between American whites and Negroes. This issue is but one aspect of the general question: *do all men have the same cognitive capacity, or are some groups more able, competent, intelligent than others?*; and opinion is divided. There are those who defend the 'psychological unity' of mankind, arguing that mental capacities are similar and that different levels of attainment between cultural groups are explicable in terms of the effects of different environmental and cultural contexts. But there is no proof that innate mental differences do *not* exist between different groups, and there are some (cf. Jensen) who argue the case for inequality of intellectual endowment.

6.2　This section continues the discussion in Block 6 by posing the additional question: able, competent, intelligent *for what?* As we have seen, different cultures require and value different skills, and develop different 'cultural aids' to stimulate them. Hence the further question: *is it valid to use our concepts of intelligence to define and analyse the cognitive capacity of all men?*

6.3

Intelligence A, B and C
group-factor analysis
multiple-factor analysis

From Block 6, Section 1.14ff., you will recall Vernon's identification of three levels of intelligence—Intelligence A, B, and C—and the two basic theoretical models of the structure of intelligence—the British hierarchical group-factor and the American multiple-factor models. In the following extract, Vernon (1969, pp. 89–90) reminds us that our idea of the content and structure of Intelligence C (and hence by implication Intelligence B) is very much a product of our culture:

The group of skills which we refer to as intelligence is a European and American middle-class invention—something which seems to be intimately bound up with puritanical values, with repression of instinctual responses and emphasis on responsibility, initiative, persistence and efficient workmanship. It is a kind of intelligence which is specially well adapted for scientific analysis, for control and exploitation of the physical world, for large-scale and long-term planning and carrying out of materialistic objectives. It has also led to the growth of complex social institutions such as nations, armies, industrial firms, school systems and universities. But it has been notably less successful than have the intelligences of some more primitive cultures in promoting harmonious personal adjustment or reducing group rivalries. Other groups have evolved intelligences which are better adapted than ours for coping with problems of agricultural and tribal living.

6.4　So, in considering apparent differences in 'intelligence' between cultures we need to consider not only genetic differences and cultural factors, but also the relevance in other cultures of our concepts of intelligence.

6.5　On the genetic side, cross-cultural considerations of intelligence highlight the context-bound nature of the heredity-environment debate. The suggested proportions of 80 per cent heredity to 20 per cent environment in the heritability of IQ have been based on populations living in the fairly homogeneous range of environments found in Britain and the USA. If the range of environments were extended to include, say, those of Indian peasants or Australian Aborigines, then these proportions would, Vernon suggests, be more nearly 50–50, or even reversed—although he doubts the value of simply adding together the contributions of genes and environment, preferring rather to stress their interaction. In the article by J. W. Berry 'Ecological and cultural factors in spatial perceptual development' (p. 112 in the second volume of the Reader), Berry hypothesises that both culture and gene pool respond adaptively to environmental pressures; but the plain fact remains that we have no way of measuring differences in genetic potential. As Vernon concludes (1969, p. 13):

gene pool

genetic potential

> . . . at the moment we can only hazard the guess that there are some genetic differences involved in some of the mental differences between ethnic groups, though their influence is probably small relative to that of the tremendous cultural differences.

6.6   Cross-cultural assessments of cognitive capacity which take account of environmental and cultural differences fall basically into three types of approach, each with a different focus, and therefore different methods. The first approach uses tests constructed and standardized in Western cultures; such an approach has been termed 'centri-cultural' because it focuses on the development of Western-type abilities. As we shall see, this first approach has some justification *within* other cultures, but hardly provides a fair basis for comparisons *between* cultures. Hence the second approach, which attempts to make such comparisons using specially devised 'culture-free' or 'culture-fair' tests. The third approach is again a 'within-culture' rather than a comparative approach, but this time the focus is on indigenous concepts of intelligence as revealed in literature, proverbs and some testing. We shall now consider these three approaches in more detail.

standardized tests

The centri-cultural approach

6.7   The use of Western tests for making comparisons between heterogeneous cultural groups is suspect on two grounds. Firstly, different groups are likely to have had different opportunities for building up the cognitive schemas sampled by the tests; and secondly, by definition such tests are unlikely to sample the full range of culturally-valued skills. However there is rather more justification for their use *within* other cultural groups. At a purely pragmatic level, there is a need for selection in education, training and employment which is particularly acute where financial resources are small, as is the case in many of the so-called developing nations. Vernon (1969, pp. 92–6), reviewing the evidence, concludes that where the abilities required are similar to those required in the West, the tests are about as valid as they are in the West against the criteria of future scholastic attainment or job efficiency. (In one sense, of course, tests in this context are an indirect measure of acculturation; in fact, Dawson found that in a sample of mine workers in Sierra Leone, a questionnaire on traditional vs. Western beliefs not only correlated highly with scores on spatial and verbal tests, but also gave slightly better predictions of job efficiency.)

6.8   The use of Western tests in cultures—and indeed sub-cultures—other than those in which they were standardized, may also be of theoretical and practical use as a tool (cf. Vernon, 1969, p. 7) 'to explore the environmental and other factors which hinder the development of abilities within underdeveloped countries or depressed minority groups'. By implication the centri-cultural approach may thus expose areas where help is needed by those wishing to make technological progress, or to be successful in the terms of the dominant culture—although it raises more general questions about the 'worth' of Western concepts of intelligence, and their promotion.

6.9   The most extensive research using the centri-cultural approach to date has been carried out by P. E. Vernon (1969), using twenty-three tests with small and unrepresentative samples (size 40 to 100) of 10–12 year-old schoolboys in England, the Hebrides, Jamaica, Uganda and Canada (Canadian Eskimos and Indians). All were being educated in the English language. The main categories of tests used were:

a   *Verbal and educational:* arithmetic, silent reading and English, oral vacabulary, rote learning and learning of meaningful information;

b   *Induction:* e.g. matrices;

c   *Concept development:* sorting and labelling, and a series of Piagetian tasks dealing with conservation and other concepts (some reported in the article by J. J. Goodnow, 'Cultural variations in cognitive skills', which is on page 97 in the second volume of the Reader);

d   *Creativity tests* of fluency and imagination;

e   *Perceptual and spatial* tests including Kohs Blocks, Witkin's EFT, and Goodenough's Draw-a-Man.

Goodenough
Draw-a-Man test

Deviation Quotient

6.10   Test results from the sample of English boys were used to derive distributions of Deviation Quotients which were used as norms for each test (English average score was 100). In this way, a profile of abilities, in terms of Western standards, was obtained for each group (e.g. Figure 4). Each boy was also interviewed, usually by a local teacher, to obtain information on his home background, schooling, interests and vocational aspirations.

Figure 4
*Profile of Median Test
Scores of Ugandan boys*
(from Vernon, 1969,
p. 184)

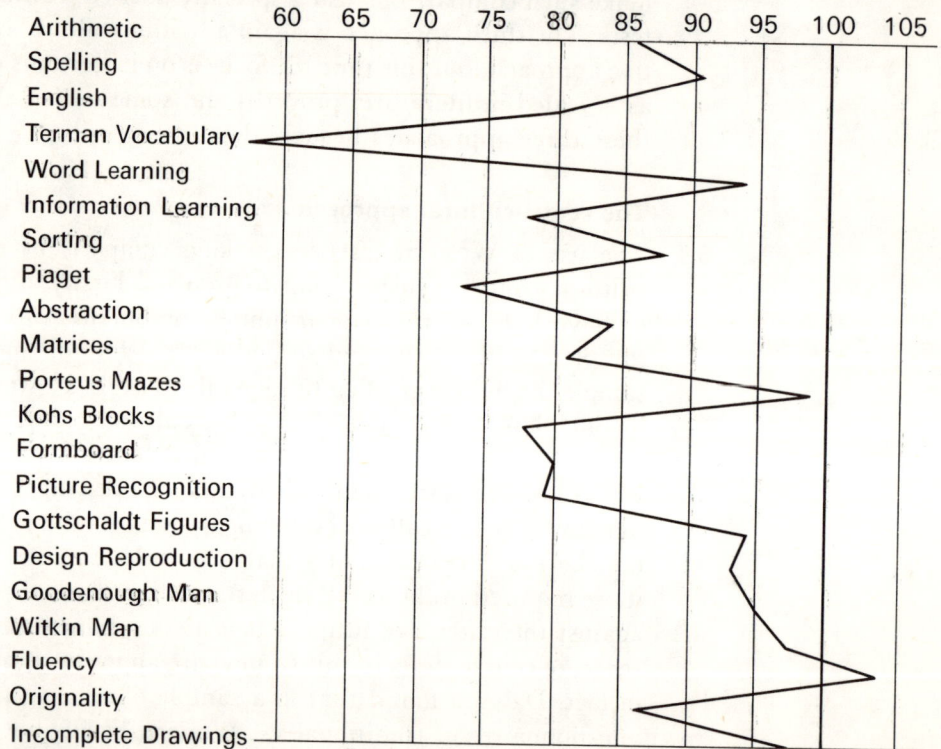

6.11   A crude summary of Vernon's results is provided by Table 7. The top half lists assessments of the factors which he considered to be the main potential handicaps in the groups he studied; below that the groups are roughly graded for all-round ability and for their performance on particular tests.

6.12   As Table 7 indicates, 'cultural stimulus' (defined by Vernon as: parents' or sibs' secondary education/books and periodicals in the home/use of library/visits to places of interest/co-operation with the school/help with homework) is clearly most diagnostic of all-round ability. But although more specific relationships can also be seen (e.g. between formal schooling and superior memorizing), few are clear-cut, especially on the non-verbal side.

Table 7   Environmental conditions and test score patterns (adapted from Vernon, 1969, p. 225)

Conditions–assessed as relative to those of the English group.	Hebridean: English-speaking	Hebridean: Gaelic-speaking	Jamaican	Ugandan	Indian	Eskimos (living in towns)	Eskimos (hostel boarders)
Socio-economic level			—		—	—	—
Providence-planfulness	+	+			—	—	—
Cultural stimulus	+		—	—	—	—	—
Language		—	—	—	—		
Adequacy of schooling	+	+	—	—			
Progressive (vs. formal)	—	—	—				
Encouragement of initiative			—	—		+	+
Home security and stability			—	—			—
Perceptual-kinaesthetic stimulation	?—	?—	—	—			
Health, nutrition			—	—	—	—	
Deficiencies in: all-round level			——	——	——	—	—
Induction		—	—		—		+
School attainments	+	+			—	—	—
Oral English and comprehension	—	—	—	—	—	—	—
Conservation			—	+	—	—	
Memorizing	+	+	+	+	—		
Fluency and originality				+		+	+
Practical-spatial	—	—	—	—	+	+	+
Perceptual	—	—		+			
Drawing			+	+	+	+	+

*A single minus indicates a slight disadvantage and a double minus a substantial disadvantage. Performance on specific tests is rated better, (+), or worse, (—), compared with the mean of all of the seven groups rather than with English norms on these tests.

6.13   Vernon admits that surveys such as his, although they may provide pointers, are 'not very effective in pinning down the factors that underly any particular deficiency, or superiority, in an ability' (p. 228). Inevitably, intensive study is sacrificed in order to obtain extensive coverage, leaving many questions unanswered. For example, did he really identify the most relevant cultural variables? His list is definitely Western-orientated (witness the definition of 'cultural stimulus'), and the influences of these variables proved to be far from constant throughout the groups. For example, the Canadian Indian and Eskimo factor-structures were similar but, whereas the Indian *g* factor correlated 0.65 with Initiative, 0.47 with Cultural Stimulus and 0.38 with Socio-economic level, the Eskimo *g* factor showed no significant relation with any of these variables, but considerable correlation with age and amount of schooling. As Lloyd (1972, p. 118) points out, it is an open question whether the relevant details of family background were assessed, or whether schooling and general experience with age are sufficient for Eskimos to override different family environments.

g factor

6.14   Finally, a general question in the 'centri-cultural' approach, and one which Vernon is very much aware of, is the extent to which test performance may be affected by factors in the testing situation itself. As we saw in Section 5, the format of the Piagetian interview may affect performance; the same is perhaps even more likely to happen with the 'centri-cultural' psychometric approach, for Western-devised tests often assume a degree of sophistication in test-taking techniques that people in other cultures may not have acquired.

Activity 7
Test-taking factors
Allow about ten minutes

What test-taking factors do you think might affect the performance on intelligence tests of people from very different cultures to our own? (For some clues, think back to your own first experiences, with, for example, the 11+; also, anything you may have noticed while administering such tests to children. You should consider, too, the cultural differences discussed in other sections of this block.)

Discussion of Activity 7

P. E. Vernon, writing from the tester's point of view, makes six main points (1969, pp. 99–100):
The following are some of the main irrelevances which the tester should seek to avoid:
1. Inability of the testee to understand the instructions, whether given in printed form or orally. Particular words or phrases may mislead or convey the wrong 'set' towards what he is supposed to do. Such misunderstandings arise not only from lack of facility in the language, or from differences in pronunciation between tester and testee, but also from insufficient attention or interest, or from anxiety.
2. With rare exceptions (notably most of the Stanford-Binet) western tests are couched in a somewhat artificial form, mainly for ease and reliability of scoring. Group tests largely employ multiple-choice, odd-man-out or even more complex item-forms, which certainly don't resemble the way we usually think, nor even how we are required to work in schools (outside the USA). Performance tests often have to be started at a signal, or other restraints are imposed. The sophisticated testee has become used to this artificiality. In printed tests he can cast his thinking into the appropriate mould, e.g. he will often read the answers before the question, and will be aware that the longest or most qualified answer is often the correct one. He develops a know-how which helps him to tackle more difficult items than when he first met this type. In much the same way the crossword addict becomes familiar with the style of clues set by the crossword author in his daily newspaper, but finds greater difficulty in tackling the puzzles in another paper. Moreover such sophistication is certainly not confined to verbal tests. The practice effects on retesting or taking parallel forms of Kohs Blocks, Formboards, Matrices and other non-verbal tests tend to be larger than with conventional intelligence or attainment tests.
3. In timed tests particularly, the sophisticated testee does not waste time on items to which he sees no immediate solution. He knows that he can probably score more by going on and returning to them if there is time at the end. He is aware of the importance of spending time on reading the instructions carefully, so as to avoid errors of Type 1. He knows that he will probably gain by guessing. But in other cultural groups there may be no stress on doing things in a set time, and the giving of answers of which one is not sure may be discouraged.
4. The western school-child has had plenty of experience of doing written work on his own, and keeping his attention on the job for quite long periods; also of competing against his fellows, or of trying hard to answer just because the teacher says so, even if the questions seem pointless. He wants to do his best to please, or to avoid criticism from teachers and parents, and he readily transfers these motivations and attitudes to the psychological test situation. In other ethnic groups, particularly when testees have not been exposed to schooling, the culture pattern may be entirely different, and the whole test situation meaningless. Competition for personal gain may be frowned upon. Important problems are discussed cooperatively with the elders of the tribe, not left to individual initiative. Even the habit (or possibly instinct) of paying attention to unfamiliar stimuli may be undeveloped.
5. The testing situation, whether individual or group, is a social situation, and often the tester is a stranger—sometimes, in western schools, a psychologist

from outside with an unfamiliar accent—sometimes, in other countries, a person of different nationality or colour. Even if he is working through an interpreter or native supervisors, he is obviously the person in charge. All of us are wary of strangers and need convincing of their friendliness and trustworthiness before committing ourselves to doing what they ask. Africans, Arabs, Asians and Australian aboriginals are particularly likely to have engrained attitudes of distrust for whites, which must interfere with their cooperation and understanding of his instructions. Also the foreign tester is naturally handicapped in understanding their attitudes and reactions, or in knowing how to appeal, or explain, to them.

6. Elements in the test materials can easily stimulate different associations in different cultures. A word or phrase, diagram or picture, may carry unintentional meanings. For example pictorial representation as such is discouraged among Moslems, so that even apart from the unfamiliarity of most Arab children with pictures, there may be inhibitions against recognising the objects portrayed.

Culture-free and culture-fair

6.14   As I have indicated, the use of Western tests for making comparisons of cognitive capacity *between* cultural groups is dubious. In response to this difficulty, special tests have been devised which try to exclude one or more of the obvious areas in which cultures vary—notably language, attitudes to speed (with reference to timed tests), and general knowledge. Historically, the development of such tests is interesting because it reflects changing views on the nature of intelligence during this century.

6.15   The first such tests were developed at a time when it was commonly thought—theoretically at least—that innate potential and the results of experience could be separated, that hereditary intelligence was merely over-laid with a cultural veneer which could be penetrated, or avoided. For obvi-ous reasons, tests purporting to do this were called 'culture-free'. One such test is Goodenough's Draw-a-Man, devised in the 1920s; it is non-verbal, has little relationship with academic subject-matter, and the figure to be drawn is universally familiar. But investigations over the years have shown that per-formance on this test is nonetheless partly dependent on cultural differences in experience with and practice of, Western representational art. For exam-ple, Dennis (1966) has demonstrated that initially low-scoring groups on the Goodenough test have improved their scores as their exposure to Western influences has increased. He suggests (cf. 6.7) that Goodenough scores may
acculturation   be treated as an index of acculturation to Western norms.

6.16   Today such a finding is no longer so surprising, since it is genereally agreed that hereditary and environmental factors interact at all stages of develop-ment. Since cultural influences will therefore always be reflected in test per-formances, the search for culture-free tests has been generally recognized as futile. The emphasis has shifted now towards attempting to construct tests which are 'culture-fair', *i.e.* which presuppose only experiences that are com-mon to different cultures.

6.17   The new name reflects the change in conception of what such tests are measuring, but the guiding principles of construction are much the same. For this reason, non-verbal tests have been much favoured as being culturally-fairer than verbal tests, with an underlying assumption that they measure the same intellectual functions. But evidence is accumulating that non-verbal tests may in fact be more culturally-loaded than verbal tests. Certainly, they are not always culture-fair—remember Hudson's challenging of the use of pictorial material (2.17–2.20), Berry's demonstration of wide culture-related differences in spatial-perceptual ability (3.17), and Goodnow's comments on spatial imaging tasks (5.16). Moreover, the assumption that non-verbal tests measure the same functions as verbal tests is highly questionable. Even though they may appear similar, we do not really know if a spatial analogies test is interchangeable with a verbal analogies test, yet this is the principle upon which some 'culture-fair' intelligence tests (for example the Leiter International Performance Scale) have been developed.

6.18   Really there seems little future for this type of comparative approach. Hypothetically there is a point at which 'culture-fair' tests might be completely fair; but by this stage, as Anastasi argues (1968, p. 253), they are likely to measure trivial functions and possess little theoretical or practical validity in *any* culture.

Reading   6.19   You should now read the article by Bernadoni (1964) 'A culture fair intelligence test for the Ugh, No and Oo-La-La cultures (p. 124 in the second volume of the Reader). Although it is an extreme parody of both this type of test and those who construct and use them, Bernadoni does make some sharp points with regard to assumptions and attitudes in the context of ability comparisons. In particular, his theme that the values of a culture are an integral component of its concept of intelligence is a central feature of our third 'approach'.
A culture fair intelligence test for the Ugh, No and Oo-La-La cultures
Barnadoni, L. C. (1964)
Reader 2, p. 124

Indigenous concepts of intelligence

6.20   As we have seen, there are good grounds for thinking that neither the centri-cultural nor the culture-fair approach is likely to sample the full range of skills developed and valued in other cultures. To be fair, as yet we lack research on the scale necessary to substantiate this doubt. But it obviously becomes questionable whether meaningful comparisons of cognitive capacity can be made across cultures. Experience so far suggests that they cannot, due to a lack of common ground between cultures—a conclusion which Berry (1969) reaches in an exploratory paper[1] on methodological frameworks for cross-cultural research, which he illustrates by referring to research into field-independence and intelligence. Basically, Berry argues that even if the Western dimension of cognitive capacity, 'intelligence', were to be replaced by a dimension based on what is agreed by all cultures to be 'intelligent', for any one culture this would only represent a fragment of their own concept of intelligence. Therefore, this new dimension would be of as little use as our present one appears to be for making universal comparisons.

6.21   As a result of this, interest in some quarters has turned to the question: what do other cultures consider 'intelligence' to be? The evidence so far is mainly confined to Africa, and two key differences from our own concept of intelligence are suggested by Robin Horton's paper (1967) on similarities and differences between African traditional religious thought and Western science.[1]

6.22   Horton is *not* suggesting that traditional thought is a kind of science; but rather that, for want of better understanding, differences of idiom have been mistaken for differences of substance. African schemas of gods and spirits have often been (mis)represented as a brand of capricious, emotional mysticism, and set in contrast with the regular, elegant, theoretical schemas of Western science. But Horton proposes that both African traditional religious thought and Western science serve the same fundamental function as tools for making sense of causality in the world; for expressing unity underlying apparent diversity and order underlying apparent disorder. Both use their schemas to transcend the limited vision of natural causes provided by common sense. Is the witch-doctor referring to spiritual agencies in diagnosing the cause of disease really so very different from the physicist referring to nuclear theory in

---

[1]*See Further Reading list.*

explaining the presence of a mushroom cloud? Or does the difference simply lie between a personal and an impersonal physical idiom? It is perhaps worth noting that Western doctors are shifting from complete adherence to the germ theory of disease, to a recognition that disturbance in social life can contribute to a whole series of bodily illnesses.

6.23   The essential difference between the two, as Horton sees it, is that African traditional thought is 'closed'. Unlike 'open' Western science, there is no developed awareness of alternatives to the established body of theoretical tenets; the traditional is sacred and protected, and to question it gives rise to anxiety because the only apparent alternative is chaos. Horton suggests that this difference stems largely from the way in which words in 'primitive' societies are closely bound up with reality. In contrast, written language in particular frees Western science from a word-thing bondage, and permits us to retain 'reality' as constant while changing the words and ideas we use to describe it. Thus we can 'get outside' our schemas and see them as such.[1] An example of taboo may make this difference of attitudes to knowledge clear. In Africa, the human corpse is generally tabooed, rejected as being not clearly within the existing animate/inanimate classification. Yet for several centuries Western scientists have used the human corpse as research material to find out more about man.

6.24   The first point from Horton, then, has to do with a 'social' emphasis in knowledge and definitions of intelligence. His portrayal of the African 'personal' idiom has much in common with Bruner's comments on the collective value orientation among the Wolof (5.17–5.20); and Gay and Cole's research (1967) among the Kpelle of Liberia provides many other examples of the way in which knowledge may be socially, rather than 'physically' or 'objectively' structured. For instance, arguments among the Kpelle are won when they are unanswerable; putting the opposition at a loss for words is more important than evidence or logic. Again Irvine (1969) writes:

> . . . African children develop a primary thought mode that perceives events and uses knowledge in a complex field of personal relationships whose organization is essentially affective. As adults they continue to use knowledge and to cognize events in this way since their theory of knowledge within a system of spiritual causation demands that they do so. This kind of cognition, which imputes purpose and force to inanimate objects, has been compared to Piaget's work on child animism; but to do this is to confuse the processes of children who think animistically because they are not fully developed with those of mature adults who exercise formal logic within the frame of knowledge at their disposal.

6.25   Irvine classified Mashona proverbs, omens and beliefs—'ground rules for intelligent and purposive acts'—in terms of the kind of knowledge needed for them to have meaning, and the consequences of non-observance. Table 8 shows that 'social' kinds of knowledge were a close second in order of importance, while, if the rules were not observed, the consequences of such action rebounded almost entirely on self, kin and community. (Irvine also demonstrated, through an analysis of wrong answers in tests given to African students in their twelfth year of education that the 'hold' of 'Western' skills was tenuous repeated failure caused regression to 'primary mode' thought.) Similarly, Wober (1974) drew on proverbs and existing literature, as well as questionnaires, to elucidate definitions of intelligent behaviour in the

---

[1]*Although Horton notes that for all the apparent modernity of his world-view, the Western layman is rarely more 'open' in his outlook than the traditional African villager; both defer to the propounders of theories (scientists and elders respectively) as being the accredited holders of knowledge.*

Baganda culture in Uganda. These definitions were characterized by a strong affective emphasis, and by a 'cautious slowness'—an attribute frequently associated with the definitions of intelligence given by traditional cultures.

Table 8   Analysis of 113 Mashona observances and omens* (from Irvine, 1969)

Consequence of non-observance on:	Knowledge required for observances and omens to have meaning					Total
	Natural objects, animals	Kin, sex, social	Personal habits, symptoms	Utilities	Seasons, time	
Self	22	19	15	7	0	63
Kin and community	14	9	3	7	1	34
Natural phenomenon	5	1	1	1	2	10
Natural objects, animals	1	2	1	2	0	6
Total	42	31	20	17	3	113

*Example: A woman must not sit on a hearth stone; her husband might die—the relationship between a natural object (a hearth stone) and the effect upon the woman's kin (her husband) is one of the fourteen responses in the natural objects/kin and community/cell.

6.26   The second point arising from Horton's paper relates to the way we define the ability to use 'abstract' thought. We tend to equate levels of intelligence with levels of abstraction (cf. Piagetian stages of development)—but does *only* Piagetian formal thought qualify as 'abstract'? Or does African traditional religious thought also qualify? The following account from Glick (a colleague of Gay and Cole) of 'informal' problem solving and classification abilities among the Kpelle of Liberia provokes some further questions (Glick, 1969, pp. 375–7):

What impressed us most is that much of the life of the Kpelle people is spent in the figuring out and solving of extremely pragmatic problems, from the adjudication of family palavers to the solution of agricultural problems. Neither of these areas has a visible codified set of rules or algorithms for solution—the processes of problem solution seem to be born of the materials of the moment, and settled within that context. Rarely, for example, in law cases is a legal precedent invoked, although there may be one which is implicit in some form of cultural expression (for example, myth or proverb). It is clear that whatever is codified is sufficiently general to allow for a wide range of solutions in the particular case.

Whether this situation derives from the absence of a shared written language or from some yet to be identified factor of cultural life, the present case seems to be that the Kpelle find themselves in the position of the 'bricoleur' (Lévi-Strauss 1966), presented with problems in particular contexts but without context-free algorithms for their solution. The bricoleur is essentially a man with a 'bag of tools' which are kept because they may come in handy. His processes of problem solution involve the deployment of this bag of tools in the concrete context, but according to no set formula and no decontextualized codified means of solution. Problems are met and solved in the ongoing process of solution without an overall plan (beyond the simple setting of a goal). A similar contrast has been drawn by Gladwin (1964,1970) in contrasting Western and Polynesian methods of navigation.

What should be noted at this point is that there is an opposition between these ethnographic ideas and those formally posed by the normal means of conceptualizing the language-cognition relationship. The ethnographic ideas suggest a treatment in terms of the pragmatics of contextualized thinking: the linguistic ideas suggest the presence of categories of formal classification systems which may override particular contexts.

Our research has led us to the posing of this opposition, and we now turn to the data that seemed to demand such an approach. . . As posed in our first experiment the problem was: If the language categorizes a set of objects in terms of a set of class names, would the linguistic classes dominate the way in which the objects were sorted out by our subjects? Accordingly, we began with a set of twenty objects, which according to both Kpelle and English belong to four classes. These were *clothes*—head-tie, shirt, singlet, trousers, and hat; *tools*—knife, hammer, file, cutlass, and hoe; *foods*—banana, orange, potato, onion, and coconut; and *containers*—cup, plate, calabash, pan, and pot. These twenty items were at first arranged haphazardly before our subjects, who were told to 'put the ones together that belong together.' Under these conditions, our Kpelle adult subjects would either isolate the items one by one or, at most, provide matches of two items. The basis for classification offered was in many cases of a functional nature—an orange and a knife would go together because the knife cut the orange. In other cases no explanation of rather exotic co-occurrences was offered. In an effort to provide greater contextual clues, we decided to constrain the possible response categories. We set out four chairs and instructed our subjects to put all the items that go together on each of the four chairs. Our hope was that as we provided information about the categorical constraints this would clarify an otherwise ambiguous situation. The results of this experiment were disappointing. Our subjects provided no startling evidence of sorting in terms of categories, or, in this instance, of sorting on any other basis. The application of more subtle measure of co-occurrence of items yielded some evidence of categorization, but at very low levels of strength.

Undaunted, we decided to constrain classification even further. In our next experiment only two chairs were provided, and subjects were again asked to put the items that belonged together on one chair. Much to our surprise this manipulation worked. In most of the cases two classes were placed together on a single chair with almost no intrusion of nonsensible items. Moreover, this effect was not due to chance or the enforced greater probability of items from the same category going together only because there were two choices. At first, this particular result seems counterintuitive—shouldn't it be the case that the four-category situation should provide the best clue to the categorical structure of a set of items having, in fact, four categories? Why, when conditions are set up that enforce a mixture of categories, do subjects tend to perform more in categorical terms? Why do their reasons for classifying the way they do shift from functional to categorical reasons as this shift is made?

To form an answer to these questions is probably to understand a lot about the way our subjects think. So, being presumptuous, I should at least like to offer an hypothesis which is testable, but which has not yet been tested. The Kpelle subject, faced with an array of familiar items, functions at first as a pragmatist. His questions are, 'How do these things relate to my experiences?' His answers are at first contextual—his experiences are not questioned to the level of linguistic categories, but only to the level of everyday encounters. As we shift the situation for the subject by forcing more and more items into proximity—a proximity that they would not ordinarily manifest—the task shifts from contextual reasoning to conceptual treatment. We are, as it were, shifting the situation from the actual to the hypothetical, from the pragmatic to the 'formal'.

6.27 In other words, for the Kpelle classifications do not exist *in vacuo*, but as descriptions of events in context (actual or hypothetical), with consequent constraints of 'reasonableness'. Glick writes: 'I believe that throughout the experiments our subjects were performing 'reasonably' [but] only in the case of the two-category situation did their criteria of reasonability match ours'. Similarly, in an earlier sorting experiment, he found that subjects would correctly sub-classify both full beer and lemonade bottles of different colours and sizes; but when empty ones were used, they would not sub-classify them, using instead the single category of garbage.

6.28   Glick's findings stress the contextualised nature of thought. They raise questions about the validity of our categories of abstract/non-abstract thought, and the division of knowledge into 'theoretical' and 'practical'; and they cast doubts on the appropriateness of the normal experimental strategy in which the test is fixed, and the subjects and their scores provide the variable element. If, instead, the experimental situation were to be varied until all subjects showed the behaviour sought (cf. Glick's use of chairs), distorted descriptions of ability from one-off tests would be avoided (e.g. if Glick had stopped with the no-chair condition). And positive statements relating behaviour to the context in which it occurs, rather than deficit statements, would be obtained.

Summary

6.29   In this section we have looked at three different approaches to the cross-cultural study of intelligence. Doubts have been raised about the value of quantitative comparisons across widely differing cultures, and reservations have been stated about the use of Western tests within other cultures. Evidence from African cultures suggests indigenous concepts of intelligence which differ markedly from our own, being much more socially and affectively defined. This evidence highlights the need to take cultural values into account when discussing 'intelligence', and suggests that we may need to rethink our experimental procedures, and our ideas of what counts as a demonstration of 'higher' forms of knowledge and ability. Glick's own conclusion (1969, p. 381) seems to me apt not only for this section on concepts and measures of cognitive capacity, but also for the whole of Part 1 of this block:

Cognition . . . is not a 'trait' held in greater or lesser degree by people. Rather, it is always an adaptive instrument, suited to the demands of an environment as seen by the subject. We cannot psychologize the subject alone without intimate knowledge of how he construes the environment that he is adapting to.

Part Two
Disadvantaged learners?

BIRMANSTOKE EDUCATION SERVICES
Smithsford Middle School

FINAL REPORT - TRANSFER TO UPPER SCHOOL

Name SMITH Paul   Age at July 19 75
                         13 yrs 3 months
Address 27 Maine Street,
        Smithsford, Birmanstoke 8

Position in family

B	B	B	G					
1	2	3	4	5	6	7	8	9

Record for period   Sept 74   to   July 75

CLASS: 1W 2J 3X 4X

NAME SMITH Paul

	attainment (1-5)	effort (A-E)	courses followed
ENGLISH	4 (32%)	D	R.A. = 10.3
MATHS	5 (19%)	D	(Schonell, 6/75)
FRENCH	5	D	En trant
SCIENCE	4 (35%)	C-	Nuffield C.S.
HISTORY	4	D	
GEOGRAPHY	4	D	
DESIGN	3	C+	
RE	5	D	
MUSIC	5	D	
PE/GAMES	1	B	

Attendance some unexplained absences   Punctuality often poor

Class teacher's comments Paul has had some remedial help in English, which has helped him slightly. He is mostly apathetic, and very quiet and contributes little to this lower band class. His parents have not come to any school function. Paul is poorly motivated. He will have to try very much harder in his next school if he is to make any progress. Member of football team.

Headmaster's comments A generally weak performance.
                                                        GT.

7 Who are the 'disadvantaged'?

7.1 This part of Block 8 is essentially a case-study of sub-cultures in England, focusing on those learners in English schools who, in recent years, have come to be commonly described as educationally, socially or culturally 'deprived', or 'disadvantaged'. The children to whom these terms are applied are typically characterized by some, if not all, of the following attributes: a home in the poorer areas of large cities; parents of low social class, with minimal formal education themselves and no contact with their children's schools; 'behind' in school attainments—but not so badly as to be classified as educationally subnormal; a 'behaviour problem'—but not so bad as to be considered maladjusted. Consider the example of Paul (see opposite).

7.2 'Disadvantage' is a relatively new word in our educational vocabulary. It has come into use as a result of concern that children from different sub-groups (usually social-class and/or ethnic-cultural) of the population do not achieve in equal proportions and that potential talent is being wasted. These are legitimate concerns; but they lead straight into a mine-field of value judgements in defining, explaining and taking action on 'disadvantage'.

value judgement

7.3 Consider the example of Paul again. He fulfils the two general criteria for the label 'disadvantaged' (i.e. poor school attainment correlated with a certain type of home circumstance and neighbourhood background). But there is no clear-cut point at which he becomes 'disadvantaged'. Home backgrounds such as Paul's are frequently judged as 'poor' or 'deficient'—which is another way of saying that they inadequately prepare the child for, and support, his school experience. But does only one certain type of home background make for success? Or is it that Paul is put at a disadvantage by an educational system which is too inflexible to accept and work with what he does have to offer?

7.4 Sections 8 and 9 will deal respectively with home and school experiences of the 'disadvantaged', drawing mainly on British research, while in Section 10 some recent developments in special programmes for the 'disadvantaged' will be considered. Thus there are geographical and, to some extent, ideological limitations to this Part of Block 8. A detailed survey of research and developments in our own culture has been chosen in preference to a more generalized comparative approach, and therefore much of the vast amount of American material on 'disadvantage'—which offers somewhat different perspectives—has been omitted. There is also the limitation that a discussion about the extent to which the causes of 'disadvantage' are located in the home or in the schools begs vital questions about the nature of education in general—the skills and knowledge and levels of achievement that are required and valued. In this block I can do no more than touch on some of these issues; other Educational Studies courses deal with them (and with the American perspective) more fully. It is arguable, however, that the adoption of 'disadvantage' as a popular educational concept has diverted educationists (including psychologists) from the more fundamental consideration of the direction of contemporary life, and the related reconsideration of the aims of education. (For an example of a development of this argument, see Friedman, 1967).

7.5 The remainder of this section looks briefly at the history of the 'disadvantage' concept. Not only does it clearly reflect changes in psychological thinking about child development and the nature of intelligence, but, more than any other concept in this course, it has direct connections with the wider political and social scene. It also shows (cf. Block 1) how conceptualization of a 'problem' determines the type of research and action undertaken. In Britain, 'disadvantage' is predominantly defined in socio-cultural terms, and we shall look first at the origins and assumptions of such an approach, and then briefly at some American influences on our thinking.

Social class and educational achievement

7.6   The response to low achievement has been slower in Britain than in the USA, where the upsurge in the 1960s of the civil rights movement swept education firmly into the political arena as an agent of social change. Until recently research has focused on analyses of social-class correlates of educational attainment. Much essential research into both home and school variables is lacking; and, compared with the USA, few monitored experimental programmes have so far been launched for children who are failing, or 'at risk' of failing, in our educational system.

7.7   In particular, since the mid-1950s research project after government report has documented the way scholastic attainment tends to coincide with social class[1]. And at all stages—whether it is the reading ability of seven-year-olds, eleven+ passes, GCE passes, length of education after statutory school-leaving age, etc.—the middle-class child tends to score better than his working-class counterpart. Swift (1968) refers to some of these 'class-chance' reports in his article, 'Social class and educational adaptation' (p. 130 in the second volume of the Reader) and summaries of the major ones are provided in the supplementary material entitled *Social Class and Educational Attainment: A Summary of Selected Research Reports, 1954–75*, which is optional reading at this point.

7.8   The Government-commissioned reports on education reveal changes in thinking about the nature of intelligence and social opportunity. The Hadow and Spens reports of the 1930s strongly sponsored streaming and selection, largely as a result of evidence from psychologists such as Sir Cyril Burt. He suggested that children could be differentiated without injustice at an early age by innate general ability. By the early 1960s the pendulum had swung the other way: the Robbins Report rejected the notion of a 'fixed pool of ability', and Edward Boyle, borrowing from Binet, stated in his Foreword to the Newsom Report that: 'The essential point is that all children should have an equal opportunity of acquiring intelligence . . .'

Plowden Report   7.9   But still the stress was on equality in *access* to education. The Plowden Report introduced a new phase by stressing both the interaction of heredity and environment in intelligence, and the need for equality of *outcome* between different social groups—which in turn required greater equality of social conditions. Hence, the late 1960s saw the growth of the Urban Aid scheme, of

Urban Aid programme
community development programmes   community development programmes set up to find 'better solutions to the problem of deprivation than we now possess'; and, in education, moves towards comprehensivization and the Educational Priority Area (EPA) policy

Educational Priority Area
positive discrimination   of positive discrimination advocated by Plowden. However, as Halsey, director of the National EPA Action-Research Programme (1968–71) points out, the EPA policy (like others before it) is arguably only a 'new formula for fair competition in the educational selection race'; assumptions about the functions of education in contemporary society remain relatively unchanged.

7.10   In essence, then, low achievement has been and still tends to be seen as a function of the social background of the child. Research has therefore concentrated on differences between children in abilities and motivation, and differences in family and/or neighbourhood conditions and values (see Section 8; and Block 3, Part 2). Such differences are often described as 'sub-cultural' in

---

[1]*Usually defined operationally according to the Registrar General's census categories for the occupation of the head of the family.*

that they represent points of discontinuity between members of a society which may nonetheless be considered in general as a single cultural group. More recently, researchers have also begun to consider low attainment as a function of the form and content of the child's school experience (see Section 9).

model

7.11   One implication of these two strands of research is that action tends to take place solely within the spheres of social and educational policy—fittingly enough, given the basic socio-cultural model of 'disadvantage'. This is the model with which we shall be concerned in this block; but you should be aware that alternative formulations of the problem of low attainment exist, which rely on different forms of research, and hence call for other types of action. The genetic model of intellectual differences, expounded notably by Jensen (Block 6, Section 5.9), calls for rather different educational programmes to those we shall be discussing here. Also there is the economic–political model, which directs attention away from the cultural context to the relationship between educational attainment and resource allocation and control. Two major British proponents of this approach are D. S. Byrne and W. Williamson, and you can read about some of their research in two Open University courses, *Urban Education* (E351) and *Education, Economy and Politics* (E352). Essentially they argue that differences between local authorities in educational capital, and what they provide with it, are a more important determinant of social class variations in attainment than the 'cultural capital' of children. However, extensive American research along these lines (e.g. Jencks, 1973) is not encouraging, suggesting that differences in educational expenditure make little difference to educational outcomes.

Reading
Social class and
educational adaptation
Swift (1968)
Reader 2, p. 130

7.12   To return to social class analysis, it is, as I indicated earlier, a useful way of describing how children from different backgrounds fare in the 'educational selection race'. But to what extent can it further our understanding of the *processes* giving rise to different levels of attainment? You should now read the article by D. F. Swift (1968) 'Social class and educational adaptation' (p. 130 in the second volume of the Reader), on which the following activity is based.

Activity 8
Social class and achievement
Allow about fifteen minutes

Q1   Does social class directly influence learning?

Q2   Are the same factors associated with educational achievement in all social classes?

Q3   How are the concepts of social class and sub-culture related?

Discussion of Activity 8

Q1   Social class is essentially a summarizing term, including a whole range of related inequalities in our social structure—inequalities of occupational and social status, power, income, educational level, housing, etc. These inequalities themselves imply some structuring of individual experience: different classes have different life-styles and ways of functioning, which influence the ease with which the child adapts to the demands of the school. Social class is thus one possible device for categorizing variables which may affect learning, *not* an independent factor that directly influences learning.

Q2   Swift argues that each social class must be seen as a unique matrix of interrelated variables, and that whether a particular factor affects achievement depends on the total class-context in which it operates (see Reader 2, p. 136). Some factors may nonetheless have a linear relationship with achievement throughout all classes—but we should not simply assume this to be so.

Q3   Both 'class' and 'sub-culture' are abstractions, and exact definitions depend on the particular author. If we take the socio-structural differences between classes to imply related cultural differences in language, socialization, educational values and so on, it might be reasonable to think of a social class as a sub-cultural group. However, caution is needed, for the broad bands of middle- and working-class are far from being culturally homogeneous. Swift notes the differences between working-class fishing and mining sub-cultures; other examples could include the Hampstead 'intellectual' vs. the Harrogate 'industrial' middle-class, Asian immigrant and indigenous manual factory workers in Bradford etc. A point of difference between 'class' and 'sub-culture' that you may have tried to draw is that 'class' holds implications of inequality that, in its strict usage, 'culture' does not (cf. 1.7). But when one group in a society becomes dominant in terms of power and resources, it also tends to become culturally dominant. Hence the notion of a *dominant sub-culture*: the group whose particular version of the culture becomes the 'official' one, its values and beliefs embodied in the laws and economy of the society, in its institutions, such as schools, and in its social structure, setting the standards against which others are judged. We shall return to the implications of cultural dominance later in this block. Meanwhile, to summarize: concepts of class and sub-culture are not congruent, but intricately related. Ethnic and regional factors especially may give rise to cultural sub-divisions of class (and class distinctions may equally sub-divide cultural groups). And in real life, of course, distinctions are even more difficult to draw because clear boundaries do not always exist either between individuals or between groups of people.

Disadvantage American-style

7.13   In the early 1960s, the poor school performance of large numbers of children, mainly urban, from ethnic and social groups other than the white middle-class, became an increasingly embarrassing political issue in the USA. Answers were required quickly to this and other social inequalities in rights and opportunities, and hopes were high that educational action would serve as a more general instrument of social change. Thus political and social factors added impetus to ideas already developing about 'disadvantage'.

7.14   The concept first emerged as 'cultural deprivation', a shorthand term for referring—or, more usually, for not having to refer too specifically—to a complex of 'home' variables believed responsible for retarding school progress. The term is curious, for it apparently implies a lack of culture—although it is arguable that all except a tiny minority of children are part of some cultural grouping, even though the extent of their enculturation may vary. In fact, as the following extract from Bereiter and Engelmann's article (1966) 'Teaching disadvantaged children in the preschool' (pp. 24–5) shows, meaning of the term was tied to a particular reference point: the existing culture and standards of American schools.

There are standards of knowledge and ability which are consistently held to be valuable in the schools, and any child in the schools who falls short of these standards by reason of his particular cultural background may be said to be culturally deprived. It does not matter that he may have other knowledge and other skills which in other contexts may be valued more highly . . . choosing the standards of the schools as a common reference point is not an arbitrary choice. The choice was made when the schools were established as the uniform means of educating all children . . . merely providing lower-class children with access to standard American formal schooling is not sufficient. They are still deprived of many important opportunities for cultural learning which are ordinarily provided through the home rather than through the school. Because of this, the children are not able to profit maximally from the opportunities that the schools provide.

Activity 9
Value judgements
Allow about ten minutes

In the above extract, what assumptions and value-judgements are Bereiter and Engelmann making about education?

Discussion of Activity 9

Three major assumptions implicit in the quotation are:

a   that schools are right to value the sorts of knowledge and ability that they do, and there is no need to question the social origin of such values;

b   that the school is blameless with regard to poor performance—the 'fault' is to be located in the child and his home rather than within the school;

c   that it is acceptable for schools to remain rigid in the face of cultural variation, and to disregard learning experiences other than those which it values.

All these assumptions are debatable. The essential point here is that such judgements are continually made, not simply by Bereiter and Engelmann, but by all concerned with deprivation and disadvantage; they are inherent in the concept.

7.15   The 'deprivation ideology' has helped to reinforce an individualized view of school failure in that the deprived child is seen as lacking certain crucial cognitive, and particularly linguistic, structures. Taken to its limit, the child is viewed as a receptacle to be filled with experience and knowledge—a view Wax and Wax (1971) have termed the 'vacuum ideology'. A less extreme position accepts the child as active in learning about the world (cf. Blocks 4 and 7), and calls for a re-orientation rather than a filling-up. But, arguably, the emphasis is still upon the skills the child does not appear to have rather than on those which he does possess. I use 'does not appear' advisedly, for quite apart from differences in intellectual skill that may exist, Glick's work (6.26 ff) exemplifies the sorts of questions we need to ask about the contexts in which skills are applied.

7.16   The action-response to the deficit view has been to provide 'compensatory' educational programmes. By definition compensatory educators tend to be environmentalists in terms of the heredity–environment debate, and IQ gain has frequently been used as a measure of the success of such programmes. But on the whole the results have been disappointing: rarely have IQ gains been very great nor, usually, have they been maintained. Such results have produced a new pessimism about the ability of education to redress inequality (cf. Jencks, 1973), and, to some extent, have added weight to the geneticists' arguments. On the other hand, they have led to debates on the value of intelligence tests as compared with achievement or performance tests, and on the relative merits of different types of programme—in particular the 'enrichment' vs. the 'structured' approach (cf. Karnes *et al.*, 1970, in Reader 1, p. 168)—and about the optimum age for intervention, and the amount of intervention needed. Most programmes have concentrated on the pre- and early school years, but increasingly this is being recognized as a second-best solution. In particular, the long-term loss of initial IQ gains has demonstrated the need for continuing support—which in turn lends weight to those critics who argue that it is not so much the child, but the school, that is deficient.

7.17   Indeed, the deficit view now has many critics as well as exponents. Many writers prefer the term 'disadvantage' insofar as they see cultural variations in terms of differences rather than deficits, but nonetheless consider that the child is disadvantaged in school by such differences. Others, as I have said, argue further that cultural differences are not intrinsically disadvantaging to learning; it is the school that makes them so. Others still have focused on a different aspect of the deficit view—namely the underlying assumption that poor children and their families do constitute some kind of cohesive sub-cultural group. Much has been written, both here and in the USA, about the *culture of poverty*, characterized as self-defeating and self-perpetuating, resigned and present-oriented, with low educational motivation and aspirations. The poor are seen as becoming habituated to poverty, developing a sub-culture of values adapted to their condition which they pass on to their children. This view has been hotly disputed (e.g. Leacock, 1971) and much seems to depend on the particular author's values and sources of information, as the following two descriptions of poor black communities in the USA show. They are both included in Leacock (1971), the first quotation appearing on p. 10; the second description, from p. 21, comes from a participant observation study. As you read them you should also consider the 'insiders' and 'outsiders' views discussed earlier (1.9).

participant observation

a   In the dregs-culture community we find the Negro philosophy of life is quite different from that of the middle-class white man or Negro. He accepts, with or without resistance, the fact that he is barred from many material successes, and as a result material values are paramount for him. He refuses to encourage his children to study because the advantages to be gained from study are too remote. We call him improvident, but in reality, he is merely a fatalist . . .

b   We see much energetic activity, great aesthetic and organizational variety, quite a number of highly patterned and well displayed behavior styles. Apathetic resignation does exist . . . but it is by no means the dominant tone of the community. Social disorganization can be found, but it occurs only within a highly structured context. Individual pathology is certainly present, but adaptive coping with adversity is more common. Positive strengths (often ignored in the literature) include the ability to deal with misfortune through humor, the capacity to respond to defeat with renewed effort, recourse to widely varied sacred and secular ideologies for psychological strength, and resourceful devices to manipulate existing structures for maximum individual or group benefit. Perhaps least expectable from popular models is the capacity to mobilize initiatives for large-scale change like the movement for local control.

7.18   The following sections on the home and school experiences of the 'disadvantaged', and examples of educational programmes designed for them, are intended to put some flesh on the bones of these view-points. I have deliberately spent some time outlining socio-cultural approaches to 'disadvantage' in an attempt to show that, while they may provide a plausible explanation of low achievement, they contain many assumptions of which we need to be aware when considering related research and provision for the 'disadvantaged' child.

8 Home experience and educational adaptation

8.1   As I indicated in the previous section, 'disadvantage' is defined in terms of failure to meet school expectations and standards, and explanations have focused on the inadequacy of home preparation and support for school experience. In this section we shall look at some differences in home experience, and how they may help or hinder successful adaptation to the demands of the school. Four main areas—material conditions, socialization, attitudes to education, and language—will be considered, bearing in mind that, to some extent, this is an artificial separation of factors.

Material conditions of the home

8.2   In 1937, Sir Cyril Burt investigated the incidence of backwardness in London boroughs and found its greatest frequency to be in the poorest areas. The percentage of backward children had correlations of 0.9 plus with variables such as overcrowding. More recent are Wiseman's studies of environmental factors in the Manchester area (Wiseman, 1968), and the findings of the ongoing National Child Development Study (NCDS), which is charting many aspects of the physical and psychological development of a 'cohort' of 16,000 children born in one week of March 1958 (Davie *et al.*, 1972).

8.3   In their first report, *From Birth to Seven* (1972) the NCDS team analysed the meaning of different environmental conditions in terms of reading attainment. Figure 5 shows that, for example, absent/shared amenities and overcrowding are equated with retardation of nine and three months in reading age respectively. (If family size is not isolated as a separate variable, as it is in Figure 5, then overcrowding is also equated with nine months' difference in reading age.) As would be expected, social class emerges in Figure 5 as a strong predictor of attainment—at age seven the difference between children from social classes I and II and those from social class V is equivalent to about fifteen months' reading age, and the study team have since reported that by the age of eleven years the differential has widened to twenty-seven months.

Figure 5
Overcrowding, lack of amenities, and reading attainment

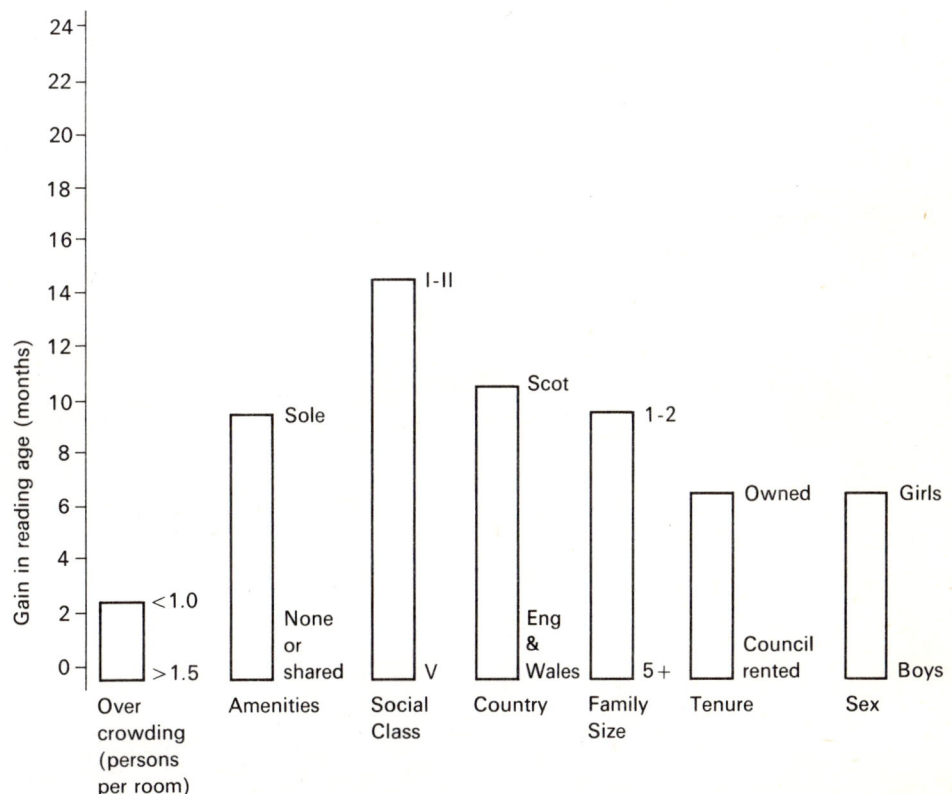

(from Davie *et al.*, 1972, Figure 14, p. 54)

8.4   The problem with such analyses is that they cannot tell us, for example, why or how a child's reading attainment is related to a lack of hot water. Obviously, a direct causal relationship would be totally naive; but it is easy to think of plausible intervening variables.

Activity 10
Material conditions of
the home
Allow about five minutes

What effects contributing to poor school performance might (a) a lack of basic household amenities and (b) overcrowding have on the child (and his parents)?

Discussion of
Activity 10

Some possible effects might be:

a   *Lack of amenities* increases the likelihood of poor physical health and hence absence from school; equally, more parental time, energy and goodwill is likely to be taken up by the 'basics' of living, leaving less time for play with the child, involvement in his education, etc.

b   *Overcrowding* is likely to reduce space and privacy for play, reading, homework, etc; one particular feature of overcrowding is bed-sharing, which increases the likelihood of disturbed sleep and cross-infection, and hence absence from or lethargy at school.

8.5   However, such suggestions are as yet mainly speculative. Moreover, isolating the effects of overcrowding, or lack of basic amenities, is somewhat false, for the two tend to go together in the context of other adverse social circumstances. In 'Born to fail?' (Wedge and Prosser, 1973), based on NCDS data on children up to the age of eleven, Wedge and Prosser offer the following definition of 'social disadvantage', which applies to 6 per cent of children, or one child in every sixteen: *a one-parent or large (5+ children) family, AND overcrowded housing lacking the basic amenities AND a low-income family.* As Figure 6 shows, about a further 30 per cent of children fall into one or two of these categories. The remaining 64 per cent are called 'ordinary'—although, of course, their family circumstances still vary. Wedge and Prosser's book is a catalogue of the range of circumstances which, even from before birth, operate against the 'disadvantaged' child more often than his 'ordinary' counterpart. Table 9 summarizes some of those circumstances relating to physical and emotional health. Some items are clearly linked with housing conditions; some have direct implications for school attainment. In general, Table 9 exemplifies part of what the Plowden Report called 'the seamless net of circumstance', which researchers are still trying to unravel.

Figure 6
Social conditions of British eleven year olds

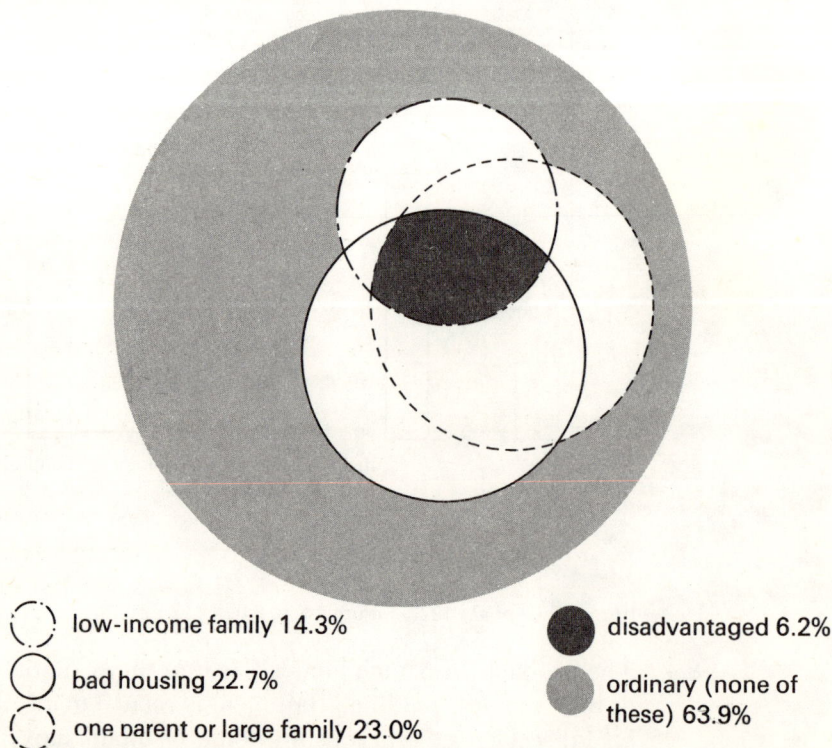

low-income family 14.3%
bad housing 22.7%
one parent or large family 23.0%
disadvantaged 6.2%
ordinary (none of these) 63.9%

(From Wedge, P. and Prosser, H., 1973, p. 17.)

Table 9   Physical and emotional health (adapted from Wedge and Prosser, 1973)

	Circumstance	Incidence in 'disadvantaged' children	Incidence in 'ordinary' children	Notes
1	Teenage mother	7%	4%	Circumstances known (along with 4+ pregnancies) to increase risk of birth complications and vulnerability to handicap; also associated with shorter height
2	Mother heavy smoker	20%	10%	
3	Antenatal visit before fifteen weeks	30%	60%	Less medical attention sought; more likely premature birth and low birth weight
4	Less than five antenatal visits	10%	3%	
5	Child absent from school 1–3 months in preceding year	9%	4%	Due to emotional disorder or ill-health. Disadvantaged more prone to infection generally, and to respiratory infection particularly. Twice as likely to have severe diseases e.g. meningitis
6	Child absent 3+ months	2%	0.4%	
7	Burns, scalds	14%	9%	Possibly connected with restricted space and poor amenities
8	Serious flesh wounds	4%	1%	
9	Vision impairment	17%	17%	Bed-sharing (53% v. 9%) increases prevalence of ear infections
10	Hearing impairment	2.8%	0.7%	
11	Speech difficulties	4.5%	1.5%	
12	Scores on Bristol Social Adjustment Guide	26% 'maladjusted' 29% 'disturbed' 45% 'well-adjusted'	9% 'maladjusted' 18% 'disturbed' 73% 'well-adjusted'	
13	Time spent 'in care' by age eleven	11%	1%	

8.6   At the same time, we need to be extremely wary of assuming that environmental conditions operate in the same way on all children. Wiseman, for example, concludes from his Manchester surveys that adverse conditions of home and neighbourhood 'have their greatest impact on the more able children', and that they are 'more effective in preventing the emergence of brightness than they are in producing backwardness'. This is all the more important, he argues, in that although IQ and class correlate positively, the parent–child IQ correlation is only about 0.5, allowing substantial differences between generations to occur. Thus, given the greater number of working-class adults, the total number (although not the percentage) of potentially bright children from working-class backgrounds far exceeds the middle-class number. Wiseman's conclusions rest on a concept of intelligence as being relatively fixed, with environmental factors depressing in particular the 'bright' child's IQ below his 'true potential'. He also makes certain assumptions about heritability of IQ. But as you read in Block 6 (sections 3 and 5), we are far from a consensus on the fixity of intelligence, definitions of environment or the contribution of genes and environment to IQ. Nonetheless, even those who disagree with Wiseman's analysis would surely agree with him that the sooner we finally disabuse ourselves of the simple equation slum = stupid, the better.

Socialization

8.7   In our society, strict training in unquestioning obedience to autocratic adults is, in general, no longer considered acceptable. Even by the age of four years old the child is a skilled social manipulator, fighting for his own interests—and parents on the whole concede him the right to do this. Hence potential conflict exists at every turn in the child's daily life: he has a continuous choice of behaving in a way acceptable to his parents (most often, mother), or not. The forms of control used by parents are perhaps the most important aspect of socialization with regard to school adaptation, for they have implications not only in terms of school discipline and the child's attitudes to 'authority', but also for how the child considers alternatives, reacts to choices and makes explanations. The studies which follow show many social class differences. However, you should remember that although some of these differences may be statistically significant, they are never of an all-or-none nature; and group means disguise quite wide variations within classes.

8.8   In an ongoing 'developmental' research project, the Newsons are interviewing a longitudinal sample of 700 mothers in Nottingham (chosen as a fairly typical urban community) to find out what they actually do in rearing their children, and how they feel about their relationships with them. The Newsons stress that they did not set out to study the influence of class—rather that class-affiliated attitudes emerged in their data as a major differentiating factor.

8.9   In terms of physical control, the Newsons found that although mothers of *all* classes smack their four-year-olds, those in Social Classes I and II were somewhat less likely to do so. There were no significant class differences in the mother's mood (calm or angry) when she smacked, or in the percentage of those believing in smacking (although their reasons for this belief varied).

8.10   More interesting differences emerge in their discussion (1970, Chapters 13 and 14) of the use of language and the mother's 'ideological' basis for control. In the various situations which the Newsons consider, the middle-class mother tends to stress *democratic reciprocity*, while the working-class mother looks to the *natural authority invested in adults*. Thus, for example, cheekiness is seen either as a matter of courtesy, or of 'who's gaffer'; lying as something the child must learn to understand, or simply be punished for; while the child's excuses of being busy when he is asked to do something may be accepted as valid on a reciprocal basis ('I like *him* to wait until I've finished doing something. So I think it's only fair for *me* to wait until *he's* finished') or, at the other extreme, his excuse may be countered with an authoritarian response ('Never mind busy, go on, get it done!). In children's quarrels, some parents prefer to let their children settle their own differences, sometimes encouraging them to hit back; other parents are more likely to intervene and arbitrate, attempting to make principles explicit, and giving the child greater incentive and practice in explaining himself in a way acceptable to adults.

8.11   The Newsons stress that the lower emphasis placed on explicit verbal communication by working-class mothers is *not* so much due to a lack of verbal facility, as has sometimes been suggested, but rather to factors of situation, attitude and emotion. This is most apparent with regard to such topics as sex;

working-class mothers are more reluctant to talk about reproduction to their children, but will discuss the *fact* of their reluctance with the interviewer. Perhaps it is even more important that they are more likely to evade telling their children the truth about sex. As Table 10 shows, this is part of a whole pattern of different attitudes towards truth, and valuations of words as the agents of truth.

Table 10   Evasion or distortion of truth with four-year-olds (adapted from Newson, J. and Newson, E., 1970, p. 501, Table 49)

	I and II	III White Collar	III Manual	IV	V
	%	%	%	%	%
False account of where babies come from	8	19	41	40	66
Idle threats of authority figure (e.g. policeman)	6	17	23	26	39
Threats to leave child or send him away (reduced sample because question not asked if child present)	10	34	29	27	30
Leaves child surreptitiously	20*	21	25	15	32
Frequent unfulfilled punishment threats	9	13	17	15	18
Other definite instances (e.g. nose will fall off if picked)	4	12	11	15	10

Notes: overall class trend significant p. < 0.001
*The Newsons comment that the middle-class attitude to language sometimes appears to be almost superstitious; in particular, they may be prepared to *act* a lie as long as they are not forced to verbalize it.

8.12   The Newsons point out that gradually the child learns that his mother may use trickery to control him, when it suits her purpose: she rarely *does* put him in a Home, for instance, or call the police. They speculate that this may be at the root of the older working-class child's frequent attitude of mistrust towards 'authority' (school, police, employers, etc.)—an attitude which, one might add, might be quite justified.

8.13   Other researchers more closely concerned with educational 'disadvantage' have drawn class distinctions in forms of control similar to those of the Newsons. Bernstein (1971)[1], for example, proposes three 'modes' of control: the *imperative*, (simply orders); the *positional* (instructions and explanations in terms of status position, e.g. 'that's silly for a boy', 'you're too old for that'); and the *personal* (instructions and explanations in terms of the particular skills and characteristics of the child, and the relation of his behaviour to other people). Bernstein offers the following example (1971, p. 158):

mode of control

Imagine a situation where a child has to visit his grandfather who is unwell and the child does not like to kiss him because the grandfather has not shaved for some time.
One mother says to the child before they go:
Mother: Children kiss their Grandpa (positional)
Child: I don't want to—why must I kiss him always?
Mother: He's not well (positional reason)—I don't want none of your nonsense (imperative).
Another mother says in the same context: 'I know you don't like kissing

[1]*Part of Bernstein's work on socialization and language codes was reviewed briefly in Block 7, Part I, but within a different framework to the discussion in this section.*

Grandpa, but he is unwell, and he is very fond of you, and it makes him very happy' [personal].

The second example is perhaps blackmail, but note that the child's intent is recognized explicitly by the mother and linked to the wishes of another. Causal relations at the interpersonal level are made. Further, in the second example, there is the appearance of the child having a choice (discretion). If the child raises a question more explanation is given. The mother, so to speak, lays out the situation for the child and the rule is learned in an individualized interpersonal context. The rule is, so to speak, *achieved* by the child. The child, given the situation and the explanation, opts for the rule. In the first example, the rule is simply *assigned* in a social relationship which relies upon latent power for its effectiveness.

8.14   The essential difference between the three modes is thus the range of alternatives given to the child in his learning of rules (including those about his own social role). Whilst it is perfectly possible for all three modes to be used in any one family, Bernstein suggested that there would be social class differences in the preferred mode of control. This suggestion was recently empirically tested for the first time by Cook–Gumperz (1973), a colleague of Bernstein's at the Sociological Research Unit of the University of London Institute of Education. Using a sample of 236 London mothers (divided into working, mixed and middle classes) with five-year-old children, she studied answers to a set of open-ended, but directed, questions based on some of the control situations which could easily arise with children of that age. For example:

mixed class

Q1   Supposing you thought it was time N. went to bed, but he/she started to cry because he/she wanted to watch something on TV. What would you say or do?

Q2   What would you do if N. brought you a bunch of flowers and you found out that he/she had got them from a neighbour's garden?

8.15   A coding grid was devised for analysing the mothers' answers according to the action that they said they would take, the linguistic appeals and situational comments they would make, and their justification for their chosen behaviour. The grid comprised twenty-four 'strategies of control', which were grouped into three sets, representing the alternative modes of control. The picture which emerges from Cook–Gumperz's analysis is far from a simple one-to-one relationship between class and mode of control. Nonetheless the data largely supports, and refines, Bernstein's theory. In particular, Cook–Gumperz found that:

a   While all three classes used all three modes, in general the middle class took up strategies within the personal, the mixed class within the positional and the working-class within the imperative mode.

b   Each group also had preferred strategies within their two non-predominant modes, e.g. the middle class preferred commands to punishment within the imperative mode.

c   *All* mothers, irrespective of class, varied their control according to the context set up by the questions. They had a similar ability to discriminate between strategies and situations, and shared similar control strategies—but they applied them differently, suggesting that the groups held different implicit theories of learning.

d   Middle-class mothers switched strategies more as they moved from question to question; their control was oriented relatively more than the other groups' to the particular attributes of the problem, the context, and the nature of their child, as well as simply to general attributes (positional/imperative). Since only four strategies were coded as imperative and five as positional, but fifteen as personal, the middle class mother obviously had the greatest range of strategies at her disposal.

8.16   Other research connected with the Sociological Research Unit provides further support for Bernstein's theory. For example, Robinson (in Bernstein, 1973) showed that the type of explanations the mother gave to the child were echoed in later years by the child himself when answering questions. Bernstein and Henderson (in Bernstein, 1973) asked mothers how they thought they would be most handicapped if they had to bring up their children without being able to speak to them. Middle-class mothers placed greatest emphasis on the personal area (e.g. Item 6: 'letting them know what you are feeling') and, within the skills area, on principles (e.g. Item 7: 'showing them how things work'). In contrast, working-class mothers put most emphasis on skill operations (e.g. Item 1, 'teaching them everyday tasks like dressing, and using a knife and fork'). In the USA, Hess and Shipman (1965) drew on Bernstein's ideas in their investigation of class differences in the teaching styles of Negro mothers with their four-year-olds. When asked how they would prepare their child for starting school, or to teach him how to group or sort a small number of toys, the mothers differed in the type and amount of information and support which they provided. As a result, on the grouping task the middle-class children made more correct groupings, and could more often verbalize their sorting principle. In terms of preparation for school, Hess and Shipman give these two contrasting examples:

a   'First of all, I would remind her that she was going to school to learn, that her teacher would take my place, and that she would be expected to follow instructions. Also, that her time was to be spent mostly in the classroom with other children, and that any questions or any problems that she might have she could consult with her teacher for assistance.'
       'Anything else?'
       'No, anything else would probably be confusing for her at her particular age.'

b   'Well, John, it's time to go to school now. You must know how to behave. The first day at school you should be a good boy and should do just what the teacher tells you to do.'

8.17   Evidence from interviews is indirect in that it only tells us what mothers *say* they would do, not how they actually behave with their children. Evidence collected in the laboratory setting is equally artificial. Nonetheless, we are beginning to have good grounds for thinking that there are indeed class-linked differences in mothers' methods of instruction and control. The real gap now lies in demonstrating how these differences take effect in the classroom. It is easy enough to speculate—for example, on the basis of their research, Bernstein and Henderson (1973) characterize the implicit theory of learning in the working-class home as 'didactic', and that in the middle-class home as 'self-regulating'. Hence they suggest that a primary school education based on personal autonomy in skill-acquisition (play and 'discovery-learning') and in developing a social role, may be inappropriate for the working-class child whose skill-learning at home has been far more specific and adult-directed, and whose social role there has been 'assigned' to him in terms of personal status, rather than 'achieved' by him. But, as yet, such ideas remain speculative.

didactic learning
self-regulated learning

social role

8.18   We shall return briefly to the relationship between class and control when considering language 'codes' in the final part of this section. For the moment, we turn to the more diffuse area of parental attitudes.

Parental attitudes and children's motivation

8.19   As Swift (1968) stresses in his article, 'Social class and educational adaptation' (p. 130 in the second volume of the Reader), although most people would agree that education is 'A Good Thing', interpretations of what it is, and what it is for, vary greatly. With regard to 'what education is for', Swift (1966) distinguishes between intellectual and social liberation (see also his article 'Social class and achievement motivation', p. 142 in the first volume of the Reader). This distinction is reflected in Morton-Williams and Finch's (1968) survey of attitudes of those who would be affected by plans to raise the school leaving age (ROSLA)—young school-leavers, their parents and teachers. Some former early-leavers were also questioned. Figure 7 shows

Figure 7 Proportion of fifteen-year-old leavers, their parents and teachers saying that various school objectives were 'very important'

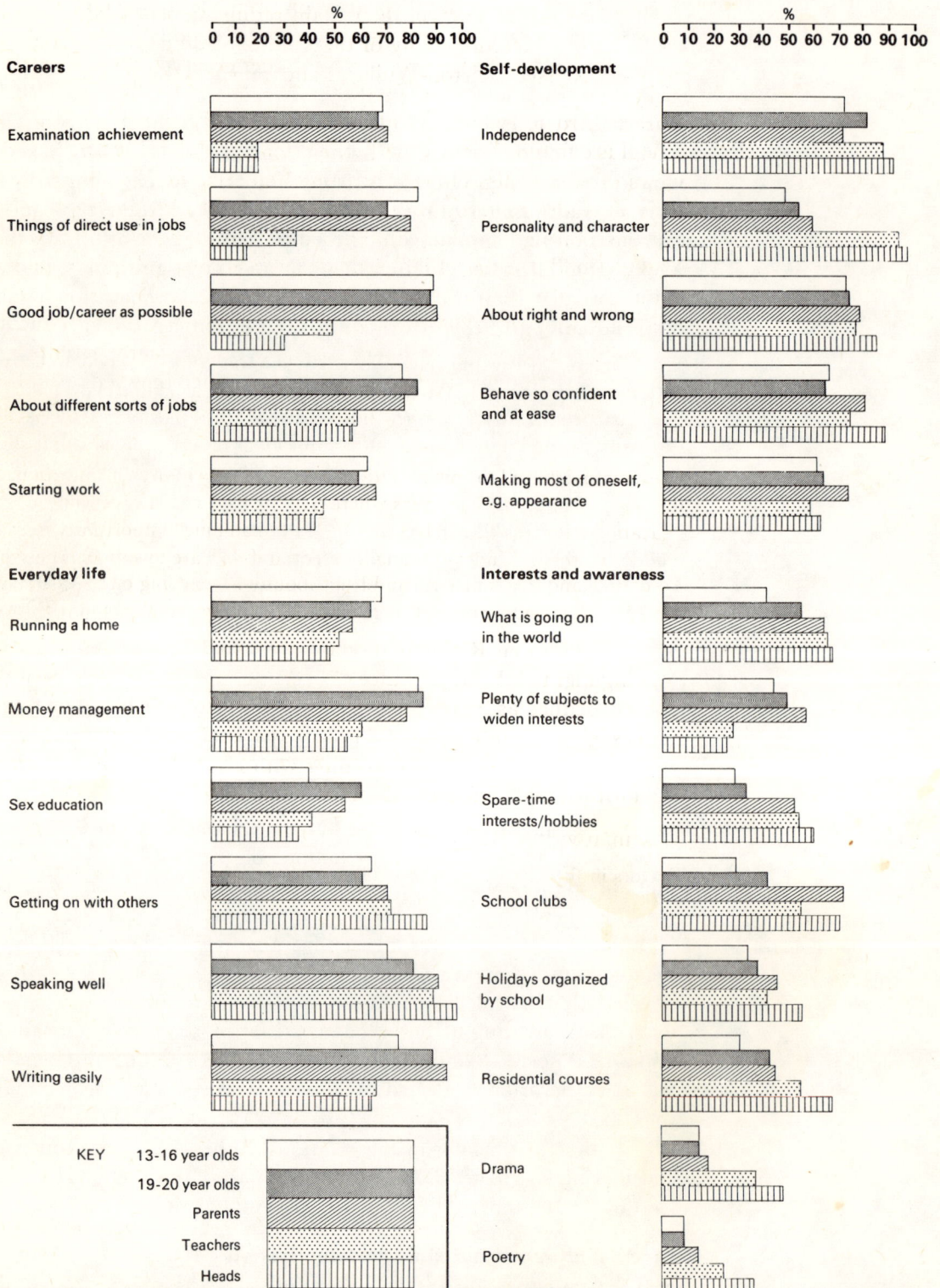

(From Morton-Williams and Finch, 1968, p. 43, Figure 6. Data obtained in individual interviews using structured questionnaires.)

considerable differences between the views of young school leavers and their parents, and those of their teachers. The former stressed vocational objectives, money management and writing fluently, while the latter valued personality and character development most highly. In Swift's terms, the parents and children look to the school for a degree of social liberation, an objective which the teachers do not particularly stress. Obviously, all sorts of questions are raised by such findings: about abilities and aspirations, possible unwarranted 'writing-off' of early-learning pupils by teachers, what the objectives of education should be, and who should decide them. The fact remains that many consumers of education have compulsorily to pay for and use a commodity which fails to meet their main requirements, is largely beyond their control and which, for many of the children results in a 'bare-bone sense of inadequacy' (see Morton-Williams and Finch, 1968, p. 240).

8.20   With regard to 'what education is', other mismatches between home and school are frequent. For example, Rutter *et al.* (1974) report on West Indian views of school discipline (which is often seen as 'lax and inefficient') and their attitudes towards pre- and infant-school play (where they place less emphasis on its importance). The latter finding is echoed by Bernstein and Young (in Bernstein, 1973), who report a class difference in conceptions about the uses of toys, with the middle-class mother more likely to be in harmony with the infant school in seeing toys as having educational significance. The general mismatch is made worse for many parents by the rapid changes that have taken place in education since they left school. Eric Midwinter (1972, p. 35), Director of the Liverpool EPA Project placed great stress on:

> . . . the crucial need for parents to understand their children's education, and
> this is particularly true in areas where parents have not always enjoyed
> educational success themselves and have not had much opportunity to study
> modern methods. Understanding is essential if they are to support the school.
> To understand they must see and hear about what is going on . . . The logic of
> it is see, understand, support. It is difficult to exaggerate this point.

8.21   Both the Plowden Report national survey and Wiseman's Manchester surveys highlighted the importance of parental support for the school's activities. Loosely defined as 'parental attitudes', this factor was based on questionnaire items such as membership of a library, parents' reading, number of books in the home, time spent in the evening with children, preferred school-leaving age for the child, initiative shown in visiting the school, etc.

Wiseman writes (1968, p. 277):

> Factors in the home environment are overwhelmingly more important than
> those of the neighbourhood or the school. Of these home influences, factors of
> maternal care and of parental attitude to education, to school and to books,
> are of far greater significance than social class and occupational level.

Similarly, G. F. Peaker writes in the Plowden Report (1967, Vol. 2, p. 181):

> The variation in parental attitudes can account for more of the variation in
> children's school achievement than either the variation in home circumstances
> [class, housing, family size, parents' education] or the variation in schools . . .
> Although the variation in parental material circumstances and parental
> education can account for some of the variation in parental attitudes it cannot
> account for very much, and leaves open the possibility that attitudes may be
> changed by persuasion.

A follow-up survey by Bynner (1972) of parents interviewed for the Plowden Report showed that, four years later, entrance to grammar and independent schools was strongly associated with support given to the child while at primary school, and that, in general, the children attending these schools again had the better-off, better-educated, more supportive parents.

8.22   The reports stress that supportive attitudes are not restricted to particular classes, although they do tend to be associated with non-manual, and especially the professional/managerial groups. Wiseman's and Peaker's arguments that parental attitudes are independent of, and more important than, class, have been criticized as being only one possible interpretation of the data.[1] But, regardless of how we choose to conceptualise the relationship between social class and parental attitudes to education, such researches have demonstrated convincingly the importance of parental support for the child's achievement at school, and have provided some of the impetus for formal and informal projects in home-school relations.

8.23   An alternative research approach to parental support is to look at family 'atmospheres' and at 'achievement motivation'. The general thesis is that parents vary in the extent to which they socialize their children into the need

n Ach   for achievement (Murray's n Ach in Block 2), by valuing and rewarding competence, high performance and independent action. The 'successful' home is often characterized as supportive and democratic, but Swift (1966 and 1968 articles in the Reader Volumes 1 and 2) and Musgrove (1966) suggest that the family life of those who are taught to achieve is no soft option—if it's tough at the top, it's also tough learning to want to be there.

8.24   Many studies have been made of the relationship between achievement motivation and attainment, but results have conflicted and it seems doubtful whether, in fact, the studies were measuring the same thing. The only thing that can be said with confidence is that high levels of achievement are associated with positive attitudes towards learning (e.g. Barker Lunn, 1972). However, research into achievement motivation, conceptualised as the outcome of certain value patterns in the home, has helped us to be more aware of the possible mismatch in values between home and school. By and large, schools value achievement in conjunction with individuality, competition, and long-term goals—whereas the pattern of home values may be towards cooperativeness, and a more immediate time-span (cf. Figure 7).

Language

8.25   Above all else, language differences have been the focus of the disadvantage debate. Another Open University Educational Studies Course[2] deals with the issues more fully; here I shall concentrate on three areas of discussion which grow out of Basil Bernstein's work on language codes.

8.26   Any discussion of Bernstein's work is fraught with difficulties, not least because over the years he has developed his ideas, changing the emphasis of

sociolinguistic codes   his theory and related research. Basically, he postulates two language codes, the *restricted* and the *elaborated*, which characterize the working-class and the middle-class (and are linked to the positional and personal family types). Bernstein first defined the codes using a rough-and-ready checklist of mixed characteristics (see the notes for Radio Programme 19 on *The Two Worlds*). Then he shifted to a definition purely in terms of the predictability of grammatical structures; for example, preference for nouns (elaborated) or pronouns (restricted), nouns allowing a greater range of modification and qualification, and therefore longer sentences.

---

[1]*See Swift (1973); and the booklet* Social Class and Educational Attainment, *which is supplementary material for this course.*
[2]*E262* Language and Learning. *See in particular Blocks 3 (Social Relationships and Language), 4 (Language in the Classroom) and 8 (Deprivation and Disadvantage?).*

8.27   Most recently he has defined the codes in semantic terms, i.e. the meaning of what people say (or write), which obviously includes grammatical structures. Thus the restricted code becomes characterized as one which is particularistic and context-dependent: much of the meaning remains implicit. The elaborated code, on the other hand, is described as universalistic and context-independent: meaning, and especially principles, are made explicit. In speculating on the origin of the two codes, Bernstein provides an interesting parallel with Bruner's comments in Section 5 on the two basic value orientations in socialization—the collective or the individual—and their implications for the child's development. Bernstein writes (1971, p. 147–8):

> An elaborated code will arise wherever the culture or sub-culture emphasizes the 'I' over the 'we'. It will arise wherever the intent of the other person cannot be taken for granted. In as much as the intent of the other person cannot be taken for granted, then speakers are forced to elaborate their meanings and make them both explicit and specific . . . In terms of what is transmitted verbally, an elaborated code encourages the speaker to focus upon the experience of others, as different from his own. In the case of a restricted code, what is transmitted verbally usually refers to the other person in terms of a common group or status membership. What is said here epitomizes the social structure and its basis of shared assumptions. Thus restricted codes could be considered status or positional codes whereas elaborated codes are orientated to persons. An elaborated code, in principle, pre-supposes a sharp boundary or gap between self and others which is crossed through the creation of speech which specifically fits a differentiated 'other'. In this sense, an elaborated code is oriented towards a person rather than a social category or status. In the case of a restricted code, the boundary or gap is between sharers and non-sharers of the code. In this sense a restricted code is positional or status *not* person oriented. It presupposes a generalized rather than a differentiated other.

8.28   Bernstein emphasizes that he does not conceive of restricted code speakers as being *deficient* in certain basic structures or vocabulary: rather, he surmises that working-class jobs, community-life and, in particular, family relationships normally constrain their linguistic choice. So he suggests that while the working-class child will rarely, if ever, use the elaborated code, the middle-class child will be more practised at being flexible, able to use both codes and switch easily between them. It is important to note here that although there has been considerable research into children's use of codes, nearly all of it has been based on experimental situations rather than in the 'live' school or family context. Again, the only 'class constraint' which has so far been systematically investigated is that of family relationships, in the context of Cook–Gumperz's research into class and control. Using a limited index of fourteen variables (use of pronouns, ego-centric vs. socio-centric sequences etc.) to define the two codes, Cook–Gumperz did indeed find that the different classes tended to realize their control modes through different codes. However, much more confirming evidence is still required to substantiate Bernstein's theory, in particular to illuminate the relationship between familial and linguistic differences and the child's performance in school.

ego-centric sequences
socio-centric sequences

8.29   Responses to Bernstein's work have ranged from the extremes of respect to those of derision. Rather than attempt to adjudicate, in the remainder of this section I shall consider three particular issues arising out of Bernstein's writings, all of which are concerned with the child's language in the school context.

Issue 1: Language as a tool for abstract thought

8.30   Bernstein proposes that the elaborated code is necessary to meet the conceptual demands of school. But while this claim draws attention to the needs language has to serve in order to be an adequate tool for thought, it runs rather ahead of the evidence. We are only beginning to find out—with some surprises—how language is actually used in the classroom (see Section 9, and Block 11). And while Bernstein assumes all aspects of the elaborated code to be functional and desirable, his critics argue that it is unnecessarily *over-elaborated*. We need to find out how much is necessary for analytic thought, and how much is merely stylistic. Is the elaborated code really 'flexible, detailed, subtle' (Jensen) or is it often 'turgid, redundant and empty, an elaborated *style* rather than a superior code or system' (Labov)?

8.31   Not that such an enquiry is easy. Firstly, an apparent lack of abstract terminology does not necessarily mean that the speaker cannot recognize, or think about, abstract relationships (although it *may* reflect a difference in 'codability'—see Section 4). Secondly, as we saw in Part 1, there are problems in defining 'abstract' thought. If it is taken as the ability to categorize and generalize, this is implied in the use of language itself, and appears to be universal—although the circumstances under which it appears may vary (see 6.26 ff). The linguist Noam Chomsky has effectively challenged the 'deprivation' theorists by putting forward a view of language as a system of rules for generating utterances. Most children learn the basic rules of their native language before school age, and in this sense virtually every child has a 'proper' language in which he is competent. For example, writers such as Bereiter and Engelmann have considered the Black American dialect to be an illogical, ungrammatical form of 'standard' English, but Labov's analysis (1970) show it is equally rule-governed: 'they mine' is the non-standard Negro English (NNE) equivalent of the standard 'they're mine'; both use a rule of contraction.

Issue 2: Situational effects on speech

8.32   Chomsky makes the distinction between underlying *competence* and actual *performance*. Evidence from a number of sources suggests that the child is not simply learning rules for generating utterances, but also rules about the circumstances in which to make particular types of utterances. This is essentially Bernstein's point; he is concerned with differences in performance rather than in competence, which he appears to accept as equal. Bernstein argues (8.28) that middle-class speech is more responsive to situational factors. However, evidence is accumulating to suggest that the speech of all children is quite strongly influenced by characteristics of the speech situation—although the 'disadvantaged' child may perceive that situation differently from his middle-class counterpart.

8.33   The main source of such evidence is American research which has been carried out, not in terms of Bernstein's codes, but in the context of differences between Standard and Non-standard Negro English, and the 'language deficit' vs. 'language difference' debate. Labov (1970) and Houston (1971), for example, have shown that black American children who appear taciturn and almost inarticulate in school or in testing, are nonetheless fluent speakers with friends and family. (They note that two, often ignored, characteristics of the urban Negro ghetto are the great pride taken in verbal facility and the predominance of verbal play among children.) Houston therefore distinguishes between School and Non-school 'Registers', the former being a limited, non-revealing language children use with persons perceived as being in authority or as wishing to study the child. The 'School Register', she argues, is adaptive and reasoned in terms of the child's perceptions—albeit maladaptive in terms of his progress in school.

Reading

The neglected situation in child language research and education

Cazden (1970)

Reader 2, p. 145

8.34   The article by Cazden (1970) 'The neglected situation in child language research and education' (p. 145 in the second volume of the Reader), which you should read at this point, opens with a brief outline of the 'deficit' and 'difference' views of language.[1] The main body of the article consists of a review of research which supports Cazden's thesis that both these views of language are inadequate insofar as they are oriented towards structure rather than patterns of use, and relate utterances to characteristics of the child to the neglect of speech situation variables. Cazden uses the term 'communicative competence' to describe how the child's perception of the situation influences his way of speaking. Since the speech situation is something teachers can change fairly easily, her review of the effects which differences in topic, task and listener(s) can make on language use is important—although you should bear in mind that her distinction between task and topic is not a clear-cut one, and these research findings are still at the tentative stage.

8.35   Returning to Bernstein's codes, an interesting piece of research is Hawkins' study (in Bernstein, 1973) of stories from five-year-olds based on a set of strip-cartoons without words.[2] This study is frequently cited as evidence in support of Bernstein's theory concerning class differences in language code, but it is possible to argue that the results are accounted for, in part at least, by situational factors. The children in the study (124 middle-class, 139 working-class) were asked to 'look at the cards and tell the story'. The results showed that the middle-class children used more nouns and associated forms (elaborated, context-independent), while the working-class children used more pronouns (restricted, context-dependent). Bernstein (1971, p. 178) cites and then comments upon two examples constructed by Hawkins on the basis of what the children said, but slightly exaggerated in order to demonstrate the most typical features of each code.

Here are the two stories:

(1)   Three boys are playing fooball and one boy kicks the ball and it goes through the window the ball breaks the window and the boys are looking at it and a man comes out and shouts at them because they've broken the window so they run away and then that lady looks out of her window and she tells the boys off.

(2)   They're playing football and he kicks it and it goes through there it breaks the window and they're looking at it and he comes out and shouts at them because they've broken it so they run away and then she looks out and she tells them off.

With the first story the reader does not have to have the four pictures which were used as the basis for the story, whereas in the case of the second story the reader would require the initial pictures in order to make sense of the story.

However, let us consider the situation. The stories were not spontaneous, but were elicited in an experimental situation; and the request was not for a written story for some absent reader, but simply for a story to be told in the presence of a researcher. Even more important, Hawkins does not say in his article whether the children knew if the researcher could see the pictures, or was aware of their content—an apparently minor point, but one that is crucial to the interpretation of the results. For if the children could reasonably assume that the researcher could see the pictures, or that he knew their content, then one could argue that the context-dependent response of the working-class children was rationally chosen and quite appropriate in the

---

[1]*See also the article by Cole and Bruner (1971) 'Cultural differences and inferences about psychological processes' (p. 165 in the second volume of the Reader).*

[2]*See the Football Picture Story Cards in the folder material for the Case-study Option.*

specific situation—perhaps more so than the context-independent response of the middle-class children, who had been taught at home to value detailed, detached descriptions as a general rule.

8.36 Consequently, the way in which the 'disadvantaged' child construes speech situations may affect the language he uses in them. The way he construes may often differ from that of the middle-class child, who is likely to share more assumptions with the teacher or tester about the speech situation and what is appropriate or 'reasonable' (cf. Glick, 6.27) behaviour in it. We do not know enough as yet to weigh situational variables against continuing family influences—but we should be aware of the child's potential flexibility in language use and the need to try and understand *his* perception of speech situations as well as our own.

Issue 3: The language valued by schools

8.37 Finally, what sort of language is valued by schools? Bernstein—and many others—would answer: an 'elaborated' language, even though as I pointed out earlier (see 8.30), we do not really know which characteristics of an 'elaborated' code are essential for optimum learning. We also lack analyses of actual classroom language according to Bernstein's terms—although the study by Hargreaves, Hester and Mellor (1975) of deviance in classrooms provides a fascinating insight. Essentially they were concerned with the day-to-day informal rules of classroom management—rules about talking, movement, time, and pupil–teacher, pupil–pupil relationships—and the ways in which teachers impute deviance (rule-breaking) to pupils. In their analysis of actual classroom events they show that, whatever his values, the teacher's language of discipline is to a large extent 'restricted' in the sense that much of its meaning lies in the context. Different statements can hold the same meaning, or the same statement can hold different meanings, according to the activity which provides its context; and only rarely are all the elements of deviance-imputation made explicit (see Table 11). More typically, only one or two elements are stated, (e.g. 'Jones!' or 'Stop it') and the pupil—and the researcher—must fill in the rest from the context and his past experience of such situations.

Table 11   Elements of deviance-imputation (based on Hargreaves *et al.,* 1975)

Element	Example
a target of the communication	Jones!
b rule being invoked	You know you're not supposed to talk while you work
c action which is being held to constitute a breach of that rule	You're talking
d conduct conforming to the rule which must be substituted for (c)	Stop it and get on with your work.

8.38 At a more general level, many teachers now agree that the insistence that pupils speak and write only in full sentences with 'correct' grammar is unnecessary and inhibiting to self-expression. Nevertheless, our standards tend to be ambivalent, especially when it comes to examinations. What is accepted, well-graded and valued in the classroom may not suit the requirements and purposes of GCE or CSE.

Activity 11
'Examination English'
Allow about 10 minutes

The following two essay extracts are quoted in the Schools Council Working Paper No. 9: *Standards in CSE and GCE: English and Mathematics.* **On one reading, how many marks out of ten would you give each extract? What comments would you make on each?**

a   **I was an honnest man, never stole an never caused a row until i lost
my job. I was a Farm Labourer getting a fair wage. I had worked at
this place for over six years, i got on well with the boss and the rest
of the workers. One year the boss died and his son took over the
Farm, he did not like Farming so he sold the farm and all its land to
some people who wanted to build a Factory. All i new was how to plough
a field and look after animals and I could not get a job in the factory.**

b   **Elizabeth Shepherd had come from a simple, rather poor family; her
father had been the vicar of the parish of Hornsey. From her
childhood she had been a good girl, a pride to her family; but to
herself she had been a failure, in looks, in talent and in wit. At the
age of 18 she had married a London merchant, she loved him dearly
and he was her soul to her, but she to him was nothing more than
someone to look after him. However by this time she had begun to
believe she could never give birth to child, for she had no confidence
in herself and it had been a long time . . . As the months passed
by the baby grew strong and beauty beamed in her bright face.**

**Discussion of
Activity 11**

The working paper cites these two extracts as the 'secure touchstones' by
which examiners using the rapid impression marking system can identify the
best and worst. The first was given two out of ten marks (less than CSE grade
4) while the second got a full ten marks, putting it high into the 'O' level
range. John Ezard (1974) reported that the Advisory Centre for Education
(ACE) showed the two extracts to a panel of experienced teachers, and to the
children's novelist, Edward Blishen. The teachers disagreed with the Working
Paper examiner's marking; they gave 2–5 and 6½–8 respectively. In contrast
to the examiner's view that the first extract was 'dead prose' while the second
showed 'poesie and mobility', the teachers commented on 'honesty and ability
to engage the reader's sympathy' and were concerned at the 'rather well-oiled
borrowing of a nineteenth century model of style and attitude'. Blishen
thought the first extract was equal in merit to the second:

> It has to my ear the true cadence of plain speech . . . Whatever seeks to
> soar, tends towards decoration, is welcomed. Fair enough. But what is
> plain, direct, relies on the force of simple language and is less than
> sophisticated in spelling and punctuation (the literary equivalents of ragged
> dress) is likely to be received quite unperceptively . . .

Summary

8.39   In this section we have looked at some of the implications which sub-cultural
differences in environment, socialization, values and language have for personality development and learning. The differences between sub-cultural
groups are obviously not so gross as those found when comparing widely
differing cultures in respect of these variables; but nonetheless we can discern
important patterns of differences between classes, even though these are not
always clear-cut, nor linked directly with research into learning and achievement.

8.40   The discussion of language here has centred on Bernstein's conception of two
linguistic codes. However three of the radio programmes in this block provide
other perspectives on language. Radio Programme 23, *Creole Dialect*, Television Programme 12, *Education in Trinidad*, and the set book by Searle, *The
Forsaken Lover*, all look at differences between Standard English and West-
Indian dialects, and the implications for West-Indian schoolchildren at
school in this country. Radio Programme 23 is closely linked with Section 10
of the correspondence text. Radio Programmes 24 and 25 together provide a
double-length feature on the question of cultural bias in children's books.
Taking up in a general way the theme of this block, cultural differences, the
programmes consider how such differences are represented to the younger
reader in words and pictures. In particular the programmes explore the ques-

tion of stereotyping; the impact on the child of what he reads: how the study of books may be used as a springboard to a more general awareness of bias and prejudice; and—last, but not least—what teachers and others can do to improve both the written materials we offer children and the ways in which such materials are used.

9 School experience

9.1   In the foreword to his book *How Children Fail* (Set Book for Blocks 9 and 10), John Holt writes (pp. 9–10):

Most children in school fail . . .
> They fail because they are afraid, bored, and confused.
> They are afraid, above all else, of failing, of disappointing or displeasing the many anxious adults around them, whose limitless hopes and expectations for them hang over their heads like a cloud.
> They are bored because the things they are given and told to do in school are so trivial, so dull, and make such limited and narrow demands on the wide spectrum of their intelligence, capabilities and talents.
> They are confused because most of the torrent of words that pours over them in school makes little or no sense. It often flatly contradicts other things they have been told, and hardly ever has any relation to what they really know—to the rough model of reality that they carry around in their minds.

9.2   The children Holt writes about in his book are mostly of above average intelligence and are 'successful' in the education system. Holt is concerned with their failure 'to develop more than a tiny part of the tremendous capacity for learning, understanding and creating with which they were born . . .'. But Holt's analysis of failure in the above extract seems to me relevant also to the failure of the 'disadvantaged' child to surmount even the early hurdles in the educational race. Arguably—for reasons we can only begin to guess at—the 'disadvantaged' child differs from his successful peers in his reactions to adult expectations and to school activities. He appears to be resigned to failure, rather than goaded on by fear of it; he will openly show his boredom, and reject confusion rather than tolerate it. In other words, if the 'disadvantaged' child comes to school less prepared than others, as Section 8 suggests, he is also less prepared to play the school game.

peers

9.3   Admittedly this is only speculation—as is so much of the writing which considers how schools may disadvantage children. But two focuses of concern have emerged: teacher attitudes and expectations (and the sources of information on which these are based), and the very nature of school activities—methods, curriculum content, learner–teacher relationships etc. We shall look at both of these areas of concern in this section, accepting that they raise many more questions than can as yet be answered, not only about the management of learning for the 'disadvantaged', but also (cf. Holt) about the nature of the education we offer all children.

Teacher attitudes and expectations

9.4   In Block 7, you read about the development of the self-concept and the self-fulfilling prophecy, with particular reference to Rosenthal and Jacobson's study (1968) of teacher expectation and pupil achievement. Their study has been severely criticized, but its theme cannot yet be dismissed. From the day he enters school the child is grouped and labelled, and his teachers develop predictions of success or failure, based on their own personal constructs, and on tests of many sorts. The teacher's sources of information will be considered shortly, but first let us consider the possible side-effects of educational groupings.

9.5   Schooling is riddled with groupings and labellings: we have streams, bands, sets, remedial groups, some tripartite secondary selection, 'Newsom children', Educational Priority Areas, even Bernstein's restricted and elaborated codes as labels. Such means of differentiating children are intended to highlight and provide for different educational needs. Often they may help the child by improving the match between teaching and intellectual development (cf. Block 3, Section 12). But equally they *may* hinder rather than help.

Activity 12
Educational grouping
Allow about ten minutes

A frequent rationale for educational grouping is that it helps the child. But consider what criticisms could be made of the grouping process in general, and what adverse effects it might have on the child's achievement?

Discussion of Activity 12

The following may be some of the points you have thought of:

a   needs are defined by those who do the grouping, rather than those who are grouped.

b   grouping focuses attention on the (perceived) qualities and potential of children, often without a critical examination of attitudes towards them, the tests used, reasons for grouping etc.

c   the basis for grouping is often arbitrary (e.g. a score of ninety on a test may be the dividing point).

d   grouping tends to give rise to stereotypes (e.g. 'the EPA child', 'boys in 4D'), which will only sometimes be true of any individual child within the labelled group.

e   groups such as 'streams' tend to be definite categories for which there are definite expectations. Human beings adapt very quickly to what seems to be expected of them in given situations (cf. Block 7, Part 2, Section 3, 'The self-fulfilling prophecy'), so if these expectations are low, we may never know whether the child could have exceeded them. The fact that moves between streams are relatively rare is often taken as evidence that 'streaming is efficient'—but is it an accurate assessment of the child, or the child meeting expectations, that makes it so? Initial streaming often takes place at the early age of seven years, and yet the variability of children and the problems of accurate assessment at this age should mean that, on test scores alone, some 20–30 per cent need to change streams during their school careers—but on the whole they don't do so.

f   Lacey's study (1966: see Reader 2, p. 58) demonstrates a relationship between streaming and the development of pupil 'sub-cultures' which may militate for or against achievement.

g   Teachers given the 'low ability' classes are often made to feel second-class themselves, doing all the hard grind with an occasional 'bright' class as a 'reward'; such views of their role may reinforce low expectations on their part.

9.6   Some forms of selective grouping are probably necessary and almost certainly inevitable at some points in mass schooling, where resources are unlikely ever to permit complete individualization of learning. The purpose of Activity 12 was simply to prompt questions about the nature of selection as it exists, and the unintended consequences it may have. Chapter 9 of Nash's (1973) study of academic self-perception in a first-year secondary school class of thirty-five eleven-year-olds, shows how acutely aware children often are of the classroom as a place of constant evaluation—evaluations by teachers and by other pupils. Pupils' estimates of their own class positions and of each others' positions correlated significantly, $r = 0.72$; and these two estimates correlated significantly with teachers' perceptions of the pupils (investigated using Kelly's Repertory Grid), $r = 0.54$ and $r = 0.69$ respectively. Nash writes (pp. 101–2):

... That others in the classroom are engaged in a continual process of evaluation has been demonstrated by the high correlation between the perception a child has of his class position and the perception his classmates have of it. It is becoming clear that within the classroom there is a commonly agreed body of knowledge about the relative abilities of all its members. These results may be taken to support the interactionist theory that children are continually engaged in forming a concept of themselves and developing a consistent pattern of behaviour appropriate to this self-concept. There is evidence that the firmer these patterns of behaviour become the more unshakeable the models of them constructed by others will be and the more power their expectations will have in confirming the others' behaviour. And the models and expectations children have of each other may be as important in determining academic behaviour as those of the teacher.

9.7   The sources of information which teachers draw on are normally two-fold. First, there are the inferences which they make about home circumstances. These are usually based on the teacher's contact with parents on the school premises, on conversations, class news, clothing and personal belongings brought to school, etc. But as Goodacre (1968, Ch. 3) showed, these inferences are very much coloured by the teacher's own social origins, and his/her pre-conceptions about 'good' homes, the relationship between social class and ability, etc. For example, Goodacre found that a Head of working class origin would be likely to consider a request from a parent to borrow a school reader as a sign of interest, but the same request to a Head of middle-class origin might be considered as a 'trivial' reason for a visit to the school. Again, infant teachers in lower working-class areas were found to think—wrongly—of their pupils as socially and intellectually homogeneous, and to lower their standards of achievement for such pupils. Goodacre also suggests that the unknown, 'unmet' parent (one in three of her sample), soon becomes regarded as the parent 'who takes little interest', without a consideration of *why* the parent doesn't visit the school—it may be because of disinterest, but equally it may be due to shiftwork, or simply diffidence about contact with the school (cf. Midwinter, 8.20).

9.8   The second source of information which a teacher uses is a wide variety of standardized tests with which to measure the child's IQ, creativity, reading age, and so on. Such test scores are often taken as sacrosanct guides as to what may be expected, and the following extract, although American, illustrates an all-too-frequent outcome of 'teaching by IQ' (Shepard, 1965, p. 22):

A teacher was working with Mary. She knew that Mary had an IQ of 119, so when she called on Mary, if Mary did not respond very quickly, the teacher would say, 'Come on, Mary, you can do this. You have to think. You know how we worked at this last week,' etcetera.

What was the teacher doing? She was pushing, stimulating, encouraging, motivating.

But when she called on Charles, who had an IQ of 71, he grunted and couldn't answer. Quickly she said, 'That's fine, son. We're glad you're here. Be sure to be here tomorrow. We are going to move the piano; you can water the flowers and clean the erasers.'

9.9   As we saw in Part 1, concepts of intelligence are very much culture-bound. Attempts to devise culture-free or culture-fair tests have met with little success, and non-verbal tests may be more culturally-loaded than verbal ones. Similarly, Torrance (Block 6) and Joncich (1964) suggest that our current concepts of creativity are, like our notions of intelligence, bound to urban industrialized science-oriented cultures; and Joncich proposes that creativity research has been much dominated by American traditions stemming from the active, restless, but rarely contemplative, independence-seeking pioneer.

9.10   Cross-cultural research allows us to see our concepts of intelligence and creativity in a wider perspective—to realize that they are the products of our culture rather than absolute and unchangeable. The appropriateness in our times of the types of intelligence and creativity we value raises a general educational question. More specifically, we are concerned here with the way such tests may discriminate against the 'disadvantaged' child.

9.11   In Block 6 (Section 3) it was pointed out that intelligence tests may be standardized on samples that are not socio-economically representative of the whole population, but are biased towards higher social groups. The influence of this may be relatively small in itself, but for the 'disadvantaged' child it tends to be compounded by test-situation factors. He is often a less 'sophisticated' test-taker (cf. Vernon, 1969, p. 98); and Cazden (1970) provides examples in her article 'The neglected situation in child language research education' (p. 145 in the second volume of the Reader) of how test scores may be improved by paying greater attention to putting the child at ease. Her article shows that different pictures of the child may be gained in different situations, suggesting that in both formal and informal evaluation, greater flexibility is needed to ensure that we see the child at his best. In an account of his teaching experience in a black ghetto school, Kohl (1970) argues that an essential pre-requisite for this is the cultivation of a state of 'suspended expectations'. He writes (pp. 21–22):

> What does it mean to suspend expectations when one is told the class one will be teaching is slow, or bright, or ordinary? At the least it means not preparing to teach in any special way or deciding beforehand on the complexity of the materials to be used during a school year . . .
>
> Particularly it means not reading IQ scores or achievement scores, not discovering who may be a source of trouble and who a solace or even a joy. It means giving your pupils a fresh chance to develop in new ways in your classroom, freed from the roles they may have adopted during their previous school careers. It means allowing children to become who they care to become, and freeing the teacher from the standards by which new pupils had been measured in the past.
>
> There are no simple ways to give up deeply rooted expectations. There are some suggestions, however: talk to students outside class; watch them play and watch them live with other young people; play with them—joking games and serious games; talk to them about yourself, what you care about; listen.
>
> In these situations the kids may surprise you and reveal rather than conceal, as is usual in the classroom, their feeling, playfulness and intelligence.

School activities

9.12   Quantitatively, the most important fact of classroom life is *talk*. As you will see in Block 11, classroom observation studies show that a remarkably large and consistent part of lesson-time (some two-thirds) is taken up by talk. Usually much more of it is teacher talk than pupil talk (or, more to the point perhaps, more the teacher talking than listening to what pupils have to say). When—as in Section 8—we ask the qualitative question: what sort of language is required and valued in schools—answers are rather less clear. However, I did suggest that although the child is unlikely to be 'deprived' in his language *per se*, the language he brings to school may not match the teacher's expectations and standards. The child's early home experience may have created a lack of interest in certain kinds of verbal behaviour, perhaps because he does not expect any benefit from them; equally, the dialect-speaking child may meet at school with a lack of understanding of his language, and a negative evaluation of it (cf. Radio Programme 23, *Creole Dialect*).

9.13   How explicitly, then, is the child helped to bridge the gap between the language he brings to school, and the language of his teachers? Radio Programme 23, *Creole Dialect*, (see also Section 10) gives an indication of how one group of teachers sets about this task, combining specific language work on differences between West Indian dialects and Standard English with explorations of cultural identity and attitudes towards dialect. These particular teachers are unusual in the sense that they form a special project team working in a field that is fairly obviously problematic. Barnes *et al.* (1971) points to a more general, yet less obvious source of mismatch between the child and the subject teacher who uses the language of his discipline (geography, science, etc.) without giving the child sufficient help to grasp his meaning. Consider the following extract from a chemistry lesson: the teacher is explaining that milk is an example of the suspension of solids in a liquid.

T   You get the white . . . what we call casein . . . that's . . . er . . . protein . . . which is good for you . . . it'll help to build bones . . . and the white is mainly the casein and so it's not actually a solution . . . it's a suspension of very fine particles together with water and various other things which are dissolved in water . . .

P.1 Sir, at my old school I shook my bottle of milk up and when I looked at it again all the side was covered with . . . er . . . like particles and . . . er . . . could they be the white particles in the milk . . . ?

P.2 Yes, and gradually they would sediment out, wouldn't they, to the bottom . . . ?

P.3 When milk goes very sour though it smells like cheese, doesn't it?

P.4 Well, it is cheese, isn't it, if you leave it long enough?

T   Anyway can we get on? . . . We'll leave a few questions for later.

Activity 13
Classroom language
Allow about ten minutes

Consider the language and experience, the frames of reference, used in the above lesson-extract.

a   What is the teacher trying to do in his first statement?
b   How successful are pupils 1 and 2, and pupils 3 and 4, in relating their own experience to the teacher's use of science language and the concept of 'suspension'?
c   What is the teacher's reaction to their attempts?

Discussion of Activity 13

Barnes comments as follows (pp. 28–9):

What is happening here? The teacher talks about milk, using his specialist language to help him perceive it as an examplar of the category 'suspension', and to free him from all other contexts and categories it might appear in. But for his pupils 'milk' collocates not with 'suspension' but with 'cheese', 'school', 'shook', 'bottle'; they perceive it in that context and his use of 'casein' and 'fine particles' signals to only two of them that some different response is expected. Pupil 1 recognizes 'particles' and, searching his experience, comes up with lumps of curd. Trying to conform to the teacher's expectation, he manages 'the side was covered with . . . like particles', his uncertainty finding its expression in the deprecatory 'like'. Pupil 2 follows this line of thought and, associating the idea of sedimentation with suspended particles, tries 'they would sediment out'. These two pupils are beginning to use the language of science to make the specifically scientific abstraction from the experience. But Pupils 3 and 4, although they are *attentive to what the teacher appears to be saying*, are unable to make this abstraction; the words the teacher has used do not signal to them which aspects of the 'milk' experience should be abstracted. Far from helping them to bridge the gulf between his frame of reference and theirs, the teacher's language acts as a barrier, of which he seems quite unaware. They are left with their own first-hand experience—'it smells like cheese'. The state of the other less articulate members of the class can only be guessed at. The teacher, frightened by his sudden glimpse of the gulf between them, hastily continues with the lesson he has planned.

The teacher teaches within his frame of reference; the pupils learn in theirs, taking in his words, which 'mean' something different to them, and struggling to incorporate this meaning into their own frames of reference. The language which is an essential instrument to him is a barrier to them. How can the teacher help his pupils to use this language as he does? Certainly not by turning away from the problem.

9.14   This gulf in language and frame of reference between teacher and pupil is reflected in an interesting article by Newton (*Times Educational Supplement*, 13.6.75) on a collection of 4th and 5th formers' essays entitled 'The importance of language in education'. Many students saw the present purpose of schools as the transmission of information, but criticized the language of teachers and textbooks for being so often incomprehensible as to make even this inefficient. Their suggestions for improvements pointed to a desire to participate more actively in the learning process and to be given greater freedom to express their own views and feelings. Such personal communication with others was seen as vitally important, but rarely a permissible use of language in school. Newton comments:

What emerges strikingly from these writings is the awareness expressed by many students of the limited opportunities for a variety of language use in school—the dominance of the written language of the pupils and the spoken language of the teacher is recognized and criticized. So is the lack of opportunity for the pupils to express their own views and opinions—even in written form . . .

Learning through talking and learning through writing are pointed to in the Bullock report as central operations in language. But the much more active part which pupils will then play in their own educative process must be recognized by teachers. Unless teachers are willing to be communicated with more often as people interested in and concerned by what other people (who happen to be their students) have to say—rather than as examiners or assessors of what has been said—and unless they are willing to allow for genuine discussion and dialogue—rather than just teacher question and pupil answer—then the Bullock Committee have recommended in vain . . .

A Language for Life, as the Bullock report was titled, was seen by these students as very different from a language for school. The task is to bring life into school. Perhaps Bullock should have asked the students how to do this.

9.15   Obviously this division between 'life' and 'school' relates not simply to uses of language but to fundamental issues of what should be learned, how, when and where. Such questions are taken up more fully in other Open University Educational Studies courses, but a few indications can be given here.

9.16   What should be learned? The anthropologist Margaret Mead, looking at differences between our concepts of education and those of contemporary 'primitive' societies, suggests that the most striking one is '*the shift from the need for an individual to learn something which everyone agrees he would wish to know, to the will of some individual to teach something which it is not agreed that anyone has any desire to know*' (in Keddie, 1973, p. 98). Mead goes on to explore the reasons for this shift in emphasis from learning to teaching; but regardless of why it has come about, the 'primitive' perspective allows us to see more clearly that it has taken place. And the implications are important. In a hunting society it would be unnecessary to convince a child that he needed to learn hunting skills, whereas in urban-industrial societies, what the child needs to learn is less well-agreed between all parties—and the emphasis on teaching detracts from the learner's wishes. It also means that teachers have to work harder as 'salesmen', persuading their 'customers' to accept what they want to sell. Not that the sales policy is always successful, as is shown by, for example, the high number of early leavers, and the estimated two million adult illiterates.

9.17 To continue the analogy, in schools such as Summerhill, Kohl's 'open class-room', or the 'free schooling' movement[1], there is a rejection of the salesman's role in favour of that of the old-style shop-assistant, with the customer being helped to find what he wants. The proponents of such an approach are united in insisting on the need to 'start where the child is', both socially and educationally, and to build on his desire to learn; to help him develop in ways meaningful to his needs and interest rather than simply imposing predetermined curricula and goals upon him.

9.18 One corollary of such an approach is that the contexts for learning need to be more varied. For at least eleven years of their lives, children are taught almost exclusively in schools, cut off from the daily round of adult life, excluded from other possible contexts for developing and practising skills. Not that it has always been so. Coleman (1972) for example, charts changes in the relative contributions of home, workplace and school to the child's education. Whereas formerly the school was auxiliary to the first two, today the work-place has become closed to the young until they enter it as employees, and the major responsibility for education is seen to lie with the school. But it may not always be so: schools are beginning to experiment with work experience and community programmes; and there is a growing trend to draw parents back into the educative process, as colleagues and partners rather than barely tolerated intruders. Both these types of change have grown out of concern for the failing child, but, of course, there are pitfalls in their implementation. The former may simply be seen as a sop to the 'non-academic' ROSLA child; the latter may be treated as a public relations exercise with little real change in home/school contributions to learning. But potentially these may be the ways of improving education not simply for the 'disadvantaged' child, but for all children[2].

Summary

9.19 Two themes run through the observations in this section: the need to consider carefully the ways in which we evaluate children, and the attitudes and expectations we develop about them; and more particularly, the need to bring the child more centrally into the learning situation, to listen to him, work from his position, help him develop and achieve his purposes. Too often we perceive the learning situation through the eyes of the teacher or the researcher rather than those of the child, yet consider again Glick's notion of 'constraints of reasonableness' and his assertion:

---

[1]*See Head (1974), especially his Introduction, for a survey of thought and practice in 'alternative' schools in Britain.*
[2]*Contexts, curricula and the role of parents, in State Schools and in 'alternatives', are extensively discussed in the Open University course E351,* Urban Education, *where the idea of an 'education permanente', i.e. education as a continuing process, is also considered. The latter is a logical extension of increasing the learners's control over what he does; throughout his life he would be able to choose when to enter, leave, or re-enter the education system.*

Two faces of Billy Casper in 'Kes' (Woodfall/United Artists film based on the novel by Barry Hines, 'A Kestrel for a Knave', Penguin, 1969).

Billy lives in a tough, depressed area. He attracts more hatred and mistrust than affection and concern. He's bored at school, where he is rejected as a failure and a loner. And his appreciation of Kes, the kestrel hawk he trains from the nest and cares for (including teaching himself to carry out systematic behaviour modification) is not really understood, even by Mr Farthing, the sympathetic teacher.

Billy doesn't want to go down the mines, but he's got little option. How could we do better by other Billy Caspers?

We cannot psychologize the subject alone without intimate knowledge of how he construes the environment that he is adapting to.

9.20   A more general theme running through both this and the previous section has been the notion of conflict or, if you prefer, mismatch, between home and school. In line with this sort of argument, some writers have portrayed the school as the agent of the dominant sub-culture (Activity 8) of the white middle-class, providing continuity of experience for children of that background while discriminating against those who differ from it in language, socialization, and values—unless they conform to the new culture[1]. The difficulty with this kind of characterization of the problem is essentially its simplicity. It has the limitation of being solely a socio-cultural model; and, as we have seen, within that framework classes and sub-cultures are not clear-cut conceptually, nor are they so in real life. Furthermore, although the relationship between social class and school attainment is well-documented, and we have evidence that significant socio-cultural differences do exist, such differences are never of an all-or-none nature, and we have more theorizing than evidence about the way in which they take effect. Finally, although such a view alerts us to ways in which, to quote Cole and Bruner (1971) 'the great power of the middle-class has rendered differences into deficits because middle-class behaviour is the yardstick of success', it tends to obscure the fact that a cultural difference in skill may be as good as a deficit if it limits the individual's ability to operate successfully in a wide range of settings.

9.21   Obviously, these criticisms of the culture-conflict hypothesis do not add up to a rejection of it. (It is after all only an hypothesis, even though it is sometimes presented as having greater substance.) Rather, they add up to a warning against accepting simple explanations for the causes of low achievement. In other words, we should not underrate the complexity of the interactions within and between the home and the school, which form the individual child's experience. At the same time, however imperfect our knowledge, we need to be active in trying to improve provision for the 'disadvantaged' child. In the next section, therefore, we shall look at some actual and proposed projects, focusing on early childhood development.

10 What's being done?

10.1   The traditional response in Britain to severe school failure has been to provide special schools and remedial departments for the fairly small percentage of school children categorized as maladjusted and slow-learning (Blocks 9 and 10). Since the late 1960s however, there has been a growing tendency to distinguish conceptually the 'disadvantaged' as a much larger group, differing in terms of perceived problems and proposed intervention—even though in practice many children so labelled are still placed in remedial classes. In all, it is a 'grey' area of educational provision. There is no clear-cut point at which a child becomes 'disadvantaged', and equally there is no clear-cut point at which the 'disadvantaged' child joins the maladjusted or slow learners—categories which in themselves raise problems of definition. Thus at times the dividing line between this section, indeed the whole of this Part of Block 8, and Blocks 9 and 10, may seem thin.

---

[1] See, for example, Jackson, B. and Marsden, D. (1962).

10.2   Drawing on Sections 7–9, we can distinguish several dimensions along which special programmes for the 'disadvantaged' may vary:

a   *Overall philosophy/aim:* within a socio-cultural framework, a number of different aims, or emphases, are possible. For example, reducing school failure (but bear in mind Halsey's point about 'new formulae for fair competition'); radical reform of education in terms of curricula, personnel, teaching methods; cultural (race and class) integration, or assimilation.

b   *General underlying view of development:* deficit vs. difference. To put it another way, the child may be seen either as lacking in 'competence', or of having the 'competence', but differing in the range and type of situations in which he applies it (i.e. performance).

c   *Area of development emphasized:* social-behavioural, cognitive-linguistic, values-motivational, or a combination.

d   *Type of programme:* formal structured vs. 'enrichment'.

e   *Personnel involved:* the combination of teachers, parents, and others, and their roles.

f   *Age-range involved:* child's age at intervention, length of special programme, long-term support and follow-up.

g   *Assessment and evaluation:* how the effects of the project on the child are monitored; whether the programme is 'action research' in the sense that it aims to feed back into further development of theory; what combination of *presage* (characteristics of children and teachers), *process* (classroom events) and *product* (learning outcomes) variables[1] is used in evaluation.

10.3   Tizard's description (1975, pp. 1–2, 5–6) of two language projects, one just finishing and one still in process, may help to illuminate some of these points of difference:

A.   *The NFER Pre-school Project (started in 1968: directed by H. L. Williams: based in five Slough nursery schools)*

The aim of the study was to evaluate a programme designed to reduce failure in the primary school. The rationale was that school failure amongst disadvantaged children is related to their failure to acquire in their early years the basic repertoire of verbal, perceptual and conceptual skills and attitudes which are needed as a foundation for school success. It was hoped that the programme would present the children in a condensed form with the kind of experiences they were presumed to have missed at home. Stress was laid on both language and perceptual training. The project was thus similar in form and rationale to the research part of the EPA pre-school programme, and some of the schools were in an EPA area. However, much clearer answers emerged from the NFER study, mainly, perhaps, because there was a longer initial period of discussion with the schools, and because all the schools carried out the same programme.

A full year was spent in discussions with the teachers concerned, preparing and modifying the programme with their help. A modified version of the Peabody Language Development Kit (PLDK) was used, together with games for perceptual training. Small groups of children were taught with the PLDK for twenty minutes daily, and the nursery staff tried to reinforce the skills taught in these sessions at appropriate informal opportunities during the rest of the school day. Perceptual training with the children took the form of a graded series of games, which were conducted by nursery assistants under the supervision of the trained teachers. The experimental group was composed of 110 children; some had only one term of the programme before moving to

---

[1]*This categorization of variables is developed in Block 11.*

primary school, others had up to six terms. All the children, together with a control group of 81 children in other nursery schools, were given an extensive battery of tests before starting on the programme and as they left it for primary school. The children were also followed up in the Primary School. At the end of their first term the Boehm Test of Basic Concepts and a measure of adjustment to school were administered. At the end of their sixth term assessments of attainments in reading and number were obtained.

The full report on this study is not yet available but some important findings have already emerged. The children in the programme made significant gains, compared to the control children who experienced a traditional nursery programme, on the Illinois Test for Psycho-linguistic Abilities (ITPA) language battery and some of the perceptual tests. However, with the exception of the Verbal Expression sub-test of the ITPA, which is essentially a test of verbal fluency, the children who had spent only two terms in the programme made gains as large as those who had spent four or more terms. The social class gap in test scores was not closed, because children in all social classes made gains of a similar size. But when tested at the age of seven there were no significant differences between the school attainments of the control children and those who had taken part in the programme. Moreover, teachers' ratings during the second half of the first term at primary school showed no difference in personal, emotional, or social adjustment, between children who had attended either type of nursery school and children without any nursery school experience.

B.   Communication skills in early childhood (directed by Joan Tough in Leeds)
This is one of the very few curriculum or compensatory projects to be derived from a prior study of development. The study in question was a longitudinal investigation of language development in middle and working-class children, much influenced by the work of Basil Bernstein (Tough, 1973). Joan Tough found that even at the age of three there were differences in both the linguistic structure and language functions of middle- and working-class children. The working-class children less often used language to report on past experiences or to predict the future, to give explanations, justify behaviour, and reflect on feelings. In addition, their mean length of utterance was shorter and their sentence structure was less complex. However, at the age of seven when language was recorded in a greater variety of situations it became clear that in certain situations, e.g. conversation with their peers, the working-class children could, and did, produce as long and complex utterances as middle-class children. But the purposes for which they used language still appeared to be different. In particular, working-class children tended not to be explicit—they seemed to assume that the listener shared their viewpoint; they tended to reflect less on their own past experiences and to use these less in accounting for the immediately observable present.

Joan Tough concluded that the educational problem is not to teach working-class children to talk more often, or in longer or more complex sentences, since all the linguistic structures are available to them if they choose to use them. The problem is rather that they have had little practice in using language for certain purposes. In professional families the mother encourages the child to make comparisons, to recall the past, and to anticipate the future, to offer explanations, and look for differences; she reads him stories, encourages creative indoor activities and imaginative play. Because the working-class child has had much less of these kinds of experience he enters school with a different set of meanings, and does not respond in the way which the teacher hopes to the tasks she sets him. Her response is usually to decide that his 'language is poor' and to try to extend his vocabulary and syntax; what he needs, however, is help in the development of verbal thinking skills. This rationale underlies Joan Tough's curriculum development research.

A year was spent with a working party of teachers preparing a draft guide entitled 'Listening to Children Talk'. This is now being used with 80 groups of teachers all over the country, in all involving about 1,500 teachers. The project depends on a very complex organization, with five full-time staff, and conferences in Leeds and in each region from time to time with head teachers, class teachers, and representatives of education authorities. The first phase of the study is aimed to make teachers more aware of the way in which the young child uses language, what features to listen for, how and when to listen, and how to appraise and make records of children talking. Each group of teachers play and discuss a series of six videotapes, and after each one try out the suggested techniques in their schools, then return and discuss as a group their findings. It is planned to evaluate the success of the project in altering teachers' attitudes to children's language at the final meeting of the first year. At this session the teachers will be asked to comment on the final videotape, and their discussion will be tape-recorded and analysed. The second phase of the project, 'Fostering Children's Language', will be carried out in the same way, but during this year ways of helping children to use language more effectively will be suggested. The essential technique which will be recommended involves the teacher entering into dialogue with the child. This, then, is no 'teacher-proof' language programme, but an attempt to bring in to the school in a systematic way the language teaching techniques of the middle-class mother, and to use them with children who have little experience of such techniques. The teachers are to be encouraged not simply to listen to the child with interest or to 'chat' with him, but to help the child to ask questions, solve problems, explore the meaning of particular situations, and in general to use language as a means of learning.

Activity 14
Language projects
Allow about ten minutes

On the basis of the brief descriptions above, jot down similarities and contrasts between Projects A and B on the seven dimensions outlined in 10.2. (The discussion of this activity is on page 100.)

10.4   In her review of British research into early childhood education Tizard (1975: see Further Reading list) is pessimistic about the expansion of early schooling alone as a means of avoiding later school failure or of closing the social class gap—although, as she also points out, this is not to say that such expansion has no value for child and mother. Accepting that without continuous rein-forcement, long-term improvements in cognitive skills cannot be achieved, she goes on to review hopeful new directions in research, which include the development of special pre-school curricula, and investigations into staff behaviour and the home learning environment (including several small-scale projects in which the child's home is visited). One-third of her book is taken up with ideas submitted by the researchers she interviewed as 'important areas for future investigation'. The four areas directly concerned with 'disad-vantage' have their roots in the research themes of sections 8 and 9 and highlight the gaps in our knowledge. They are as follows:

a   *Assisting young disadvantaged children to acquire skills*—evaluation of remedia-tion through one-to-one teaching, parental involvement in school, home visit-ing, TV, classes for adolescents, and specific educational strategies; 'process' as well as 'product' evaluation.

b   *Characteristics of the socially disadvantaged child*—broadly motivational; need to study children's cognitive skills in action in natural settings outside the school and/or testing situation, and how these skills may be transferred into these situations.

c   *Transmission of disadvantage*—language, control, maternal teaching styles, learning at home.

d   *Adapting the school to the disadvantaged child*—teachers' assumptions about what children know and how they learn; comparison of maternal and school teaching strategies; investigating the 'hidden pedagogy' of the school.

10.5   Turning now to the broadcasts that accompany this section, Television

**Discussion of
Activity 14**

		Project A	Project B
a	**Overall aim**	To reduce school failure	To reduce school failure
b	**View of development**	Clearly 'deficit'—providing condensed training to develop 'missing' skills.	'Difference'—linguistic structures available but used for different purposes; approach at variance with common view of teachers—thus project aimed at teachers also
c	**Focus**	Development of language forms and perceptual skills	Development of *uses* of language, rather than of linguistic structures
d	**Type**	Fairly structured	Very loosely structured; emphasis on teacher–child dialogue
e	**Personnel**	Nursery teachers and assistants, consulted in the development of the materials used. No parents.	Nursery and infant teachers, closely involved in the ongoing development of project's suggested techniques. No parents.
f	**Extent**	2–4+ nursery terms. No follow-up into primary schools, where initial gains had apparently been lost.	During period age 3–6; no follow-up intervention
g	**Evaluation**	Extensive pre- and post-testing, linked to social class, i.e. *presage/product* evaluation	Still evolving. Main emphasis on classroom *process*—project not 'teacher-proof', as is A. Evaluation of changes in teachers' attitudes as well as in children's development.

Programme 13, *Nurture Groups,* and Radio Programme 23, *Creole Dialect* look at two quite different types of project. A brief description of the aims and work of each is given below, and you should try to read this before tuning in to the broadcasts bearing in mind again the dimensions outlined in 10.2. Further background information and activities based on the programmes are provided in the Broadcast Notes.

Nurture groups

nurture groups   10.6   'Nurture groups' provide the setting within a number of ILEA (Inner London Education Authority) infant and junior schools for a programme of compensatory work at an early developmental level. The project started in 1970 with two groups; by 1975/6 the number of groups had grown to twenty-five, most of them infants. The groups are aided financially by the ILEA 'Children with Special Difficulties' scheme: they are run autonomously, and therefore all differently, by the schools concerned, but Marjorie Boxall—an educational psychologist with ILEA based at the Woodbury Down Child Guidance Unit, and the original proponent of the 'nurture' approach—has taken much of the responsibility for co-ordination, development and evaluation. In the following article, Boxall (1976) outlines the concept of nurture and the work of nurture groups.

Reading

The nurture group in the primary school
Boxall (1976)

Part I—The nature of the problem—The emotionally deprived child at home and in school

In our schools there are increasing numbers of children who are unable to meet the expectations and demands of an ordinary nursery or infant class. Their personal organization is poor and they show learning and personality problems to varying degrees, and in many cases behaviour problems which may lead to disruption of the group. The more severe problems are usually referred to the school psychologist or child guidance clinic. Psycho-therapy is rarely the answer for the problem lies in the total situation. For this reason many of the children are referred on to special schools for ESN and maladjusted children. Others remain in the ordinary schools and stress and frustration may continue for both teacher and child.

Many of these children live under conditions of hardship and stress. Those taken into the nurture groups usually come from overburdened and fragmented families where relationships are often eroded and strained, and frequently destructive and even violent. There may be sudden and unexpected loss and change. The mother is under stress and this may affect her interaction with the child in different ways and at different stages. At the baby stage she may be too preoccupied or depressed to mirror her baby's mood and involve herself in his interest in the world. Even where this is a satisfying time for both, the sustaining interaction between mother and child may be abruptly impaired by sudden harsh weaning, often coinciding with neglect and restriction on exploration and play. Often, at this point, the child is handed over to baby minders with the additional fragmentation of experience this involves. The crucial loss to the child is likely to be the continuing interaction through which he internalizes concepts, skills and controls as he is helped to explore relationships and to control his own behaviour. In some families life is less damaging, and the problem may be mainly the management of assertive and resistive behaviour. This is especially so where the parents were themselves deprived children, for their emotional resources are slender and the stress of demanding difficult children can be the last straw. The parents become over-controlling, punitive or erratic in their behaviour, and what they say and do may be more relevant to their own feelings and mood than to that of the child.

Not surprisingly, children deprived in these ways are likely to grow up with a confused impression of themselves and the world, little sense of stability and sequence, a fragile identity and poor self control. Where life is damaging and frustrating, aggression is frequently a major problem, though some children become inhibited, while others barely function.

School

School, whether infants or nursery, is based on the assumption that the children will be essentially biddable, will have some understanding of the teacher's expectations, and will be willing to entrust themselves to her. It pre-supposes that they are sufficiently well organised to attend and follow through what is required without being constantly reminded, and that they already have some sense of time through the comfort and security of routines established at home. They are, furthermore, in a large group situation and must therefore be able to wait when this is necessary, to give and take with the other children, and to have some tolerance for frustration. School will therefore continue a learning process which under normal conditions begins in the home.

These assumptions are not necessarily true for severely deprived and disadvantaged children. They do not accept the teacher as a trustful and reliable person, and do not attach themselves with confidence; they cannot engage with the situation and they do not learn. The problems may well worsen and are often cumulative as the gap widens. Many teachers intuitively recognise the essential immaturity of the children and try to help them at an earlier level. The strain of meeting such a wide range of social, emotional and intellectual needs is, however, too great. The teachers become like the children, eroded and fragmented, and even sometimes resistive and hostile.

The orientation of the nurture group

The problems of these children are assumed to stem from the erosion of early care in families suffering from severe social fragmentation and stress. In particular, constructive interaction with the child is lost. This leads to a weakening of trust because of the reduced expectation of support, the impoverishment of early experiences, and a failure to work satisfactorily through early developmental stages.

In the nurture group the teacher and helper attempt to put in this early care and support by re-living with the child the missed nurturing experience of the early years. The model is that of the mother and her young child and the method is correspondingly intuitive; teacher and helper 'feel into' the early years and interact with the child as a mother would, within a relationship of trust.

The setting is a domestic one, and there is scope for unhurried experiences at a baby and toddler level. The nurture teacher allows the child to 'be' and helps him to 'do'; she holds him close and gradually lets him go as he becomes increasingly able to manage on his own. The general guideline to which the teacher and helper return whenever in doubt is: 'This child is 3, 2, 1 year old, in some cases even younger. I will be for him and do for him as I would my own child at that age'. This guideline is reassuring, it yields insights into the needs of the children, and from it flows a wide range of techniques.

Part II—A practical guide to the nurture approach—Identification and selection of children for the nurture group

Selection of the children is made by the school. The criterion is the child's inability to engage himself constructively in the day to day life of the class because of inadequacies which seem crucially linked with impoverishment and crippling in the early years. The problems cover a wide range and include children who are unresponsive and never speak, those who are violently aggressive and disruptive and in the extreme case are markedly anti-social; others again who are unhappy, unventuring children, sometimes severely maladjusted.

The problems are many and varied but they appear to fall roughly into five main groupings, each with a different emphasis of need. There are no hard and fast lines between these and there is much overlapping. These groupings are described in detail in Appendix I [not reprinted here] where illustrative case histories are given.

Organisation within the school

Nurture groups have on average twelve children at any one time, but it is usual for many more children than this to go through the group in a year. A classroom or hut in the playground is provided, with comfortable domestic furnishings as well as work and play space. The relaxed setting is particularly important.

The nurture concept is implemented in different ways. Most schools have a full-time group, always with some interaction with the main stream of the school from the beginning. Some have modified the basic pattern and admit some of the children part-time, while in others virtually all the children are part-time. One practice is to use the nurture facilities for new entrants felt to be 'at risk'. Whatever the approach, it is generally felt that some children need a full-time nurturing experience, while others *actively benefit* from greater contact with the ordinary class. The difference between full- and part-time nurture groups is thus largely one of emphasis.

The aim of the nurture teacher is to get the child back into an ordinary class. He must therefore not feel, nor be felt by others to be, separate and different from the other children in the school. (This in any case would be illogical because he is not a special category of child. He is in one way or another at the extreme end of a continuum of disadvantage, often multiple, and in the ordinary class there are other children who are not very different from him.) For these reasons the nurture group is ideally a flexible resource with give and take, of both teachers and children. This is fostered in different ways. In some schools the nurture children register with their class and are helped to feel part of that class, while in many schools extra children regularly go into the nurture room to play, often before school begins. In some schools the class teacher has breakfast with the nurture group from time to time, or joins them for a birthday party; and the nurture teacher might go into the ordinary class to help her children settle in.

Sympathetic rapport and good communication between the nurture teacher and class teacher is clearly important, each sharing an interest in the children's progress, and reinforcing what the other one does. Logically this implies a nurture orientation throughout the school, with all the teachers and ancillary staff in sympathy with the approach. The key person in fostering this is the head teacher, but it depends on a good working partnership with the nurture teacher, and good relationships throughout the school as a whole.

In general the trend in schools with established nurture groups is towards an earlier nurturing experience for more children provided by a wide range of people, with more intensive work on a part- or full-time basis within the nurture group, and an increasing involvement with the parents, often in a nurturing relationship.

The activities and management of the nurture group
The account which follows is the collated material from infant and junior groups where a high proportion of the children were impulse-dominated and had serious problems of aggression. It attempts to bring out the pre-school principles involved but the emphasis varies from one group of children to another, and in some schools is more explicit than in others. As in a well functioning ordinary class the organisation of the teacher does not obtrude, so in the nurture group the detailed programming is not always apparent. Similarly, the baby behaviour of the children, so vivid in description, takes its place as a transient, though intense and meaningful, developmental need. This might suddenly change, and a child who has been wearing a doll's nappy one moment might be absorbed in a constructional game the next. To a visitor the most striking feature might well be the easy and intimate physical contact between adult and child, the warmth and intimacy of the family atmosphere, and the good-humoured acceptance, with control, of infantile and resistive behaviour.

Mums ....come .paint. play. on .Tuesdays p.m

Nurture Groups

The general approach

The relaxed setting facilitates close physical proximity and eye contact, and the children become aware, often for the first time, of the teacher's face, her expression, her gestures, the tone in her voice and what all these mean. Eye contact is of crucial importance and for most of the children can be established many times during the day when they are collected together in the 'home' area, for here they are able to settle and wait and attend.

In many different ways a close tie with the teacher is established and maintained, and individual supports are built in because the children are too immature to manage on their own. Thus there would be little or no choice at first because the children have no experience from which to exercise it: toys and work would be handed to the children and instructions and requests would be specific to each child, spoken quietly in close physical proximity, with eye contact and touch where necessary. Teacher and helper settle the children down individually, giving simple reminders, with much repetition. Every task, however simple, is broken down into stages; the complexity for the child is anticipated and the task programmed accordingly. A running commentary is a help to the child in internalizing the experience and the expectations. There is stress on tidying up and putting away in a particular place, because this basic training helps to build organization into the child; it gives him security, confident anticipation and prediction, and a sense of time. A slow pace is important for the children need time to assimilate each stage; if taken on too quickly they become confused. Formal work, too, is programmed, and for most of the children this is at a very early level with much repetition. The children, who are distractible in an ordinary class, can give intense attention to simple activities. The language of the teacher, as with the mother, instinctively matches the level of activity of the child. At this stage various braking techniques are built in, familiar and reassuring routines that control his unchannelled energy, so that he waits and takes in and feels satisfied. In ways such as these the child's experiences and behaviour are monitored as by a mother. The child is 'held' by the teacher. She controls the situation so that he is not bombarded, and gradually lets him go as he becomes able to manage on his own. Stress in this situation is reduced and the problems are considerably relieved, particularly temper tantrums.

Children whose difficulties arise from inadequate and ill-organized experiences respond well in this secure setting. Others however have been managed erratically or punitively at home and present more serious behaviour problems. Control of their behaviour is an urgent priority and the strict and unremitting attention given to this in the groups is crucial. Desirable behaviour is constantly stressed and gets a positive response; undesirable behaviour like fighting is as far as possible ignored. The teacher's expectations are made absolutely clear and the only pressures in the group at this stage are those concerned with personal control. This is straightforward training: 'I see, I grab, I don't get'. Their teacher is always fair and gives a reason and they quickly accept and begin to enforce the group code.

Food

Food embodies the mother–child relationship and has enormous symbolic value. The timid tearful children from the beginning experience the family-food occasions as loving and caring; it is part of their fabric of support and contributes to a sense of comfort and well-being. For the particularly aggressive children it may at first be the only thing to which they attend, and in attending to the food they must attend to the teacher. This may be the first time that eye contact is established, the first time they notice the teacher as a person rather than a thing.

For such children, who may be virtually unmanageable, food is a powerful 'holding' situation affording maximum control, and provides an important opportunity to build in vital learning experiences: holding back, waiting, sharing, choosing, taking turns, giving up for others, and tolerating frustration. As one of the helpers put it: 'We have a tremendous palaver for a tiny piece of toast'. Food may be 'breakfast', perhaps no more than half a slice of toast and a choice of jam, or biscuits with their milk; some groups have food only when they bake. It is particularly important in the early days. In this situation, as in all others, the primitive behaviour which immediately becomes apparent in many of the children is not aggression but greed; if this is not anticipated, the children will grab at anything, and push and fight. This greed is controlled, as it is with toys and other experiences, by exposing the child to the situation in tolerable stages and not giving a surfeit; and praise is lavish, for the children are greedy also to be the best and to get the most praise. The timid and inhibited children need encouragement to eat and to play, and if the situation is not controlled will get left out. They are reassured by the firm control and the teacher–child equilibrium they see established seems to help them to be more assertive.

Infantile needs and interests

All the children, whatever their problems, need and have available to them early infantile experiences. In both infant and junior groups a general need, in some cases intense, is for close physical contact with the teacher and helper. In some this seems primarily a need for reassurance and affection. In others, particularly West Indian children, there seems to be a need for attachment at the baby stage and repeatedly teachers and helpers describe the baby-like curl of the feet and the aimless babylike movements as they push their hands into her. They lie on her lap and are cradled and rocked, stroke her hair and ruffle it; they play with her hands and her feet and her jewellery, and love to comb her hair. Some slip into baby babbling sounds and crawl on the floor. They babble and jabber and want to be picked up, or move in an unco-ordinated way, fingers in their mouths; they pick things up and give them to their teacher, or bang them noisily on the table. An interest in their bodies and its functions is shown by most of the children and for some of them this is absorbing and all consuming and they describe their experiences in uninhibited detail. They readily identify with each other at this level and live each other's anecdotes with avid pleasure. With the older children this is more than an interested monologue; it is the stuff of their conversation. They have uninhibited sexual interests too. For most of the children these interests are childish and ephemeral and lively involvement one week has disappeared without trace by the next. In a few cases these interests are sophisticated and reality based, and the imbalance in the children is an added source of stress.

Play

These early developmental stages link with the initial lack of interest shown by the children in small dolls and cuddly toys. They seem to move on to doll play, and caring for the dolls, only after their own need for affection has been met; in the early days it is *they* who wear the doll's nappy and suck from the bottle, and play babies together and comb each other's hair and feed each other. But big stuffed dolls and animals are important to them at an early stage and are the object of fierce love and hate. Later they become members of the peer group, and a monkey in a junior school sits at the table pencil in hand, wearing an anorak and doing his sums, while in another junior school a bear is given a book to read.

Many of the children have a dominant need to mess with paints, clay, water and sand and enjoy this at a sensuous level. Even junior children spend hours at the water trough, blowing bubbles and experimenting, and they enjoy scooping the sand; they like to feel it and let it run through their fingers. Many of them spend days in repetitive play, perhaps doing a simple jigsaw over and over again, or crashing the cars, or pushing and pulling heavy toys in the playground. For many children play is at first solitary, but they get used to playing alongside each other, and then gradually parallel and then co-operative play develops, becoming more elaborate as they act out their feelings and take on roles. Occasionally the solitary and repetitive play seems a defence, a retreat from the world when it is all too much. Whatever the level and nature of their play, teacher and helper are available to share the experience, guide, put in ideas, or participate in the role demanded by the child. At other times it may be more important for the children to play quietly at their feet as they talk, running their cars up and down their legs.

Behaviour management: learning self control

Most of the children in the nurture groups have serious behaviour problems; others, who at first barely function or are babylike in their behaviour, go through a phase of fights and tantrums. Many of these outbursts have the quality of infantile fury and, as with a very young child, the incidents which provoke them are trivial, but they can be difficult to manage because the children are big and strong. The orderliness and organisation of the day gives shape to the children and directs their energy, and after an upset it is easy to re-engage the child in a known and comfortable routine. It is usually possible to avoid an escalation of trouble by intervening at the first sign of niggly interference; and if the group gets 'high' the children can generally be calmed by drawing them into the 'home' area and waiting until everyone is quiet and still. Many fights and tantrums can be averted because the children are dominated by immediate perceptions and it is easy, therefore, to attract their attention to something else. All these are techniques that a mother would use with her very young child. Talking about the situations that provoke trouble, and the angry feelings they have, is important. They are taught not to hit out when they have these feelings, but to keep them inside and show their annoyance in a more grown-up way; and they talk about other people's feelings and the sort of things that hurt. Verbalising in this way slows the children down; they are able to reflect on what they would otherwise do impulsively and in this way begin to internalise the teachers's expectations and controls. Games centring on facial expressions and feelings also help, as does looking at themselves in a mirror because it draws their attention to their unrecognised feelings and what the teacher requires. In the early days of a difficult group a high risk period is first thing in the morning, especially on Mondays, and a little 'breakfast' at about ten o'clock has a markedly stabilizing effect. If a fight does break out the children move away from the disturbance and carry on with their activities as they have been trained to do, so they don't suck in the anxiety and get inflamed by the aggression, and the fight itself is as far as possible ignored. A child in a temper tantrum would be held until it was all over, or left to pummel the cushions; the teacher would talk about what had happened and when it was all over would explain about the sort of behaviour she likes, and only then would she give reassurance and support. Difficult groups seem to reach a crescendo of bad behaviour, fights and tantrums and then calm down and consolidate.

Becoming independent

The children in the groups are closely identified with the teacher and helper and this attachment is seen in the use of transitional objects. The children wear her jewellery, her poncho, and the more immature children particularly love to wear her scarf. Sometimes the teacher leaves them with something from herself, a symbol of her support and control, to help them manage their feelings when she is not there. This might be a ribbon, tied on the child's wrist when they go on an outing, or the comment when she leaves him alone 'Keep my seat warm, I won't be long'. Sometimes the children give a clear indication of their need from the teacher for comfort, support and control. Thus a girl, running from the play centre when she saw her teacher leaving at the end of the day, asked for a kiss. Her teacher kissed her lightly because she had just put on her lipstick and didn't want to leave this on the child's face. 'No, kiss me properly', said the child. 'I want your lipstick.' Some of the children, typically the more aggressive ones, are excessively dependent on their teacher and in these cases separation might be initiated by the teacher. A nine year old boy would lie for long periods on his teacher's lap and follow her everywhere. She brought in a large 'gonk' which she cuddled on her knee during story time and the child cuddled up by her side. After a few days, if his teacher didn't have the 'gonk' he would go looking for it and would sit with it and plait its hair and tie its arms round his wrist. It became important to him, satisfied his need for his teacher, and he didn't go on her lap again.

Mother's day

These early needs and infantile protests are a stage only in the children's development, and as they become less dependent they move out into wider and more complex experiences. Choice is extended, frustrations are built in in ways which are tolerable, and satisfactions are delayed. Games are played, often before an anticipated pleasure, and these centre on basic cognitive skills, the building in of confidence and a sense of identity, and a feeling of personal worth. Visits out are planned, but the children are always carefully prepared, are told what to expect and how to behave and may practise in school beforehand. A favourite visit is to the helper's or teacher's home for a drink and cake and chat. Their interest in the teacher and helper is insatiable; they love hearing about their children and ask for the same anecdotes over and over again. In the groups otherwise they play a great deal, and the teacher and helper would take on roles as required by the children and thus contribute to the development of their play. Talking, too, is very important, when baking with the helper or sitting round the ironing board while she irons, or as a family occasion over their drinks. Lastly, all the children attempt some kind of directed work, though in some cases at a very early level, and this may quickly take up a substantial part of the day.

Adult relationships as a model

Within this setting the relationship between the teacher and helper is of great importance, for this is often the only opportunity the children have of seeing constructive interaction between adults. For this reason they talk together, sharing views, show concern for each other and acknowledge courtesies, and have fun and laugh. It is usual for a peripheral man to be involved, perhaps the headmaster or caretaker, or helper or teacher's husband; they are seen to support and value the teacher and helper, they may romp with the children or tell them a story, or take them off for a game in the park.

Parental involvement

Some parents are never seen; others call in at school from time to time and may take part in the school day; others again are regular attenders at parents' parties. In some schools everyone in the family is invited to these parties and it is usual for the nurture group children to prepare the food and hand it round. The importance for the children is that home and school visibly become one, for they see parent and teacher talking together on equal and friendly terms; for the parents, many of whom are difficult to reach, it is an occasion when they are valued for themselves, not just because they are parents of the children. The teachers run these groups and many important themes arise in discussion. Most of the parents accept the shared nurturing between home and school, and remark with relief and pleasure on the children's progress.

Measuring progress

We know the children are making progress when pleasing becomes the child's reward, and satisfactions are experienced in terms of human relationships; when guilt develops; when they begin to show more concern for each other, share spontaneously, and can accept disappointments and tolerate frustration; when a sense of humour comes and they can laugh at themselves; when concentration improves and they become calmer, friendly, confident, and much much happier.

It is of interest that the children seem to experience the steps they take towards social maturity as lessons. They seem aware that the teacher is providing a learning experience and get a sense of satisfaction and achievement when they succeed. This is perhaps best expressed in the words of an infant child, a particularly aggressive girl, who remarked to the helper one day: 'Miss, it's a nice feeling, being good'.

Not surprisingly, with this developing maturity, is a marked improvement in their academic work.

Getting back into the ordinary class

This more mature behaviour is built in through a close interaction with the teacher and helper; it becomes part of the child and is not imposed from without. He becomes better able to participate in a normal group without direct help and as soon as he seems ready to manage is tried out for short carefully planned periods. This may be before he is quite ready, because there comes a critical point when greater progress is made in the ordinary class even though there may be difficulties at first. Boredom is a good indication that he is ready to move on. The situation, however, has to be carefully watched by everyone because his experience is still shaky and inadequate, his personal control flimsy, and anxiety and panic may quickly surface.

Although some children settle in their ordinary classes with very little direct help, and in some cases may take the initiative to go, others need the kind of help that a supportive mother intuitively provides for her child when he goes to school for the first time. Thus the child is already familiar with the inside of the class and has the expectation that nice things will happen there; he knows exactly what to expect and what he is required to do and is not put into a situation where he may fail; and if another child is being 'weaned' at the same time, they may well go off together. In some cases the teacher or helper would help the child prepare his things and might go with him to his class to settle him in. The less secure children might take something from her, perhaps a special pencil or her bracelet, as a comfort and support. The receiving teacher makes him welcome, and when he returns to the nurture group, perhaps for tea, he talks about what he has done and may show his work. All these supports help the child over the difficult early stages.

Conclusion

The work done in the nurture groups is based on the attachment of the child to the teacher and helper at an early level of dependency. Through interaction at this level an expectation of on-going support is established: the child trusts, and teacher and helper build on this trust, and make demands on the child because he is safe in their keeping. The approach is essentially an educational one for it is forward looking and is concerned, not with problems, but with growth and the conditions which facilitate growth.

Clearly, the younger the child, the better the support provided by the whole school and the greater the involvement with the parents, the more likely is this growth to be initiated and maintained.

Those who have been closely concerned with this project have no doubt at all the growth can be initiated and maintained, and well-being fostered, in children whose life situation is difficult and often appalling beyond belief. The underlying hypothesis is a very simple one and can be implemented intuitively without the need for a lengthy theoretical training. Anxiety is thus reduced and teacher and helper are enabled to draw maximally on their own resources and are not inhibited by the feeling that somewhere there are experts who know better. They are self-reliant and secure in their own autonomy, have a clear sense of direction and a rough idea of the possibility of success with the different kinds of problems. The work is thus approached with confidence, and because they give themselves fully to the children, energies previously unused are mobilized. Teacher and helper have a greater sense of identity in their role, feel they are using themselves fully and, like all parents, they grow with the children. All work hard, but the stress is constructive, not frustrating; they give a great deal but are amply rewarded by the affection of the children and the joy of their progress. The relief to the other teachers is considerable and a greater sense of community develops in the school.

Supplementary Service to Schools (Waltham Forest)

10.7   The Service was set up by the Outer London Borough of Waltham Forest in 1970 to provide local schools with teachers who were free to work specifically with pupils of West Indian origin, both on language difficulties and in the more diffuse area of language, colour and identity. Reprinted below is a statement of the aims of the Service, produced in 1975, when it was still felt that the role of the Service was neither fully understood nor accepted in many of the schools, even though the Service teachers have tried to encourage discussion among staff about the nature of dialect and its acceptability in the classroom.

10.8   In 1975, the Service had a staff of some twenty-five teachers attached singly or in pairs to primary, junior high (age 11–14) and senior high schools in the area, where they teach for four and a half days a week. Friday afternoons are spent at the Service's Headquarters, which acts as a resource/supplies centre and as a discussion forum. Pupils are selected on the basis of observation and informal interview; contact with parents varies widely. In some schools a special room is set aside for the Service. The Service has not so far carried out a full-scale formal evaluation of its own work, being dubious of the value of such an exercise since the school situations they are working in are so varied, and the results of their work not readily quantifiable.

Supplementary Service to Schools

The aims of the Service:

The Supplementary Service was established to provide teachers who could offer specific help to the pupils of West Indian origin in the Borough's schools.

The policy of assimilation of immigrant groups into mainstream educational provision had clearly not worked for many West Indians, and the concern expressed at national level prompted a review of the situation in this borough.

Bernard Coard's polemic, 'How the West Indian child is made educationally sub-normal in the British School System', gave extra publicity to an ILEA report which disclosed the disproportionally high numbers of West Indian pupils in E.S.N. Schools and tended to make critical appraisal of techniques of assessment the focus of the debate, centering attention on the most obviously failing or failed child. The investigation locally revealed a more general pattern of under-achievement and indicated that even children who had made satisfactory progress in their early years of schooling experienced difficulty in sustaining impetus. This reflected ultimately in the comparatively low examination achievements of many students and a poor representation of West Indian Students in the high status examination groups or taking advanced level subject courses. There were disturbing reports of worrying behaviour both of a disruptive or withdrawn nature, and many other pupils (at all age levels) were defined as lacking motivation. The conclusion was that some form of provision, 'positive discrimination', was required and that it would be extended across the whole ability and age range. This provision would take the form of programmes of work designed to supplement and not replace the work of the classroom and any remedial help the pupil required. This last point was considered to be important for a number of reasons.

Minority groups can be defined as at a disadvantage in comparison to members of the majority group in a number of different ways. The West Indian minority have a historical affinity to this country but differ significantly in many aspects of their culture, i.e. language, and most obviously in terms of their colour. Research evidence has shown that many very young black children tend to identify with the colour of the majority population. This may be 'natural' in view of the impact of the models they have around them, reflected by the media, school etc., but reflects a 'negative' attitude to their own colour which can only be psychologically very damaging. Therefore to create a situation where West Indians see themselves as 'failures' or in the black' backward readers group can only help to reinforce the negative aspects of their self image, when in fact the role of the Supplementary Service teacher is, where possible, to reinforce positive attitudes to self and identity.

The attached description of the work of the Service will perhaps make clear where the work of the Supplementary Service teacher will complement and reinforce teaching rather than *replace* any other provision (such as remedial reading) deemed necessary.

The discussions about West Indian pupils threw up a number of comments about language and speech. Reference was made to pupils who were reluctant to speak, who were unintelligible, or who used ungrammatical forms of written and spoken English.

The assumption seemed to be that West Indian English was an adoption of Standard English with an imperfect use of its grammar. Some research indicated that a more accurate explanation was that West Indians use a modification or adaptation of Creole. Creole has its own syntax, lexes and phonology, and speech items which appear 'un-grammatical' to Standard speakers are in fact completely accurate in Creole form.

Further, many of the children, because of their socialisation within a West Indian speaking environment, were discovered to have some proficiency in using a 'purer' form of dialect, but that strong constraints against using it in public situations (i.e. school) were in operation.

The development of a language programme specific to West Indian pupils therefore involved some interesting considerations:

a   The attitude of West Indians to dialect. This could be interpreted as strictly expedient, or as a reflection of ambivalence rooted in historical experience. (There is evidence of West Indian devaluation of dialect [slave talk] and that to speak a Standard variety—e.g. Standard English or Standard Jamaican is 'better'.)

b   Whatever the interpretation of (a) the implication of constraints could be to put the child who is more familiar and therefore more at ease with a dialect form of speech at a serious disadvantage within the classroom situation.

c   It was possible that current English teaching practice might not result in pupils arriving at a good working knowledge of the two distinct language systems.

d   A denial or non-recognition of two significant aspects of identity (colour and language) could result in a situation whereby for emotional and psychological reasons it was impossible for many pupils to perform adequately within the school situation.

The aim of our programmes of work is to provide:

i)   Carefully structured language work to enable the pupils to understand the differences between Standard English and their dialect.

ii) Experience and practice of all the forms of language function and communication that are required within the school situation.

iii) Familiarity with and enjoyment of aspects of Caribbean culture (folk stories, literature and music) and an opportunity to explore and use dialect.

iv) Information and knowledge about the Caribbean, and an opportunity to learn about significant and successful black people, past and contemporary.

The work is designed to be relevant to the individual needs of pupils at all school age levels and all abilities. Raising standards of literacy is implicit in the aims of the work and materials are carefully selected and compiled with this end in view. The Supplementary Service teacher can offer a great deal of help to the unsuccessful reader, particularly if it is given in conjunction with other specialists, but as the outline of the work suggests, poor reading is not the only criterion for inclusion into the withdrawal groups.

11 Postscript

Reading   11.1   To conclude your work on this block you should read the article by Cole and
Cultural differences and   Bruner (1971) 'Cultural differences and inferences about psychological pro-
inferences about   cesses' (p. 165 in the second volume of the Reader). You will find that this
psychological processes   article both summarizes and extends some of the material in both Parts of
Cole and Bruner (1971)   Block 8.
Reader 2, p. 165
                           11.2   Essentially Cole and Bruner provide an elaboration of Cazden's theme that
                                  more attention needs to be paid in psychological theory to the effects of
                                  situational factors on the performance of skills. Drawing on both cross- and
                                  sub-cultural research, they conclude that cultural groups differ more in the
                                  range of situations to which they apply their skills than in the nature of the
                                  intellectual competences they possess.

                           11.3   But although Cole and Bruner suggest that in terms of psychological theory,
                                  cultural differences in intellectual competence may be only superficial, they
                                  acknowledge that, for example, equivalent grammatical competences in Non-
                                  standard Negro and Standard English are not equally valuable in terms of
                                  access to power/prestige/resources. As I pointed out at the beginning of Part
                                  2, it is impossible to write in a cut-and-dried, objective fashion about 'disad-
                                  vantage'; by definition, value-judgements and debates about wider social and
                                  educational issues are involved. Discussing 'disadvantage' should therefore
                                  prompt us to question more closely the education we provide for all children,
                                  youth and adults.

Glossary

Acculturation (enculturation) 6.15 The process whereby an individual acquires, the norms, values, attitudes, beliefs and skills of a particular culture.

Anthropology 1.7 A branch of social science concerned with the study of man in all his aspects. Together with the social structure and functions of societies (social anthropology), it concerns itself with the biology and ecology of man and the development of human cultures, both individually and as a whole, including man's use of tools, methods of agriculture etc. Anthropology has usually restricted itself to the study of small and relatively 'simple' societies, or parts of societies, which can be studied in small units by direct observation. Anthropology is distinguished from sociology by its broader scope and by its different, although overlapping, methodologies and theoretical foundation.

Carpentered world hypothesis 2.9 This hypothesis advanced by Segall, Campbell and Herskovits, states that, if people's visual inference habits are affected by their surrounding environment, people who live in environments full of man-made objects consisting of straight edges, right angles and cubes (e.g., square rooms and houses) would be more susceptible to the Sander Parallelogram and the Müller–Lyer illusions. This would be due to their inference habits concerning the appearance of right angles extended in space. This hypothesis has been tested and found to be partially true, although other factors also influence illusion susceptibility and inference habits.

Codability 4.12 Used here for the degree to which a category or class of entities can be named quickly and consistently with familiar and usually short single words, e.g. cars, discos, etc.

Cognitive style 1.10 An individual's preferred mode of problem solving, thinking, or learning. Such preference may be specific to many or only a few tasks (see Block 5).

Community development programmes 7.9 Programmes designed to increase the identification of individuals with their community, or to create a community where none previously existed. Educationally, efforts are being made to create community schools which serve the needs of children and adults within a defined area. Attempts are being made to involve the school with local people and local needs to a far larger extent than is often the case in secondary schools where the pupils come from a wider area.

Compensatory education 1.8 A general category of educational strategies which set out to compensate for presumed deficits in school pupils. These deficits are seen as residing either in the child himself, or in the characteristics of the home and the out-of-school environment.

Conservation 5.3 The ability to understand constancy of quantity in situations where objects or substances are made to look different. For example, if a length of string is wound into a ball, the length does not vary (conservation of length): if a ball of clay is rolled into a sausage-shape, it still has the same volume (conservation of volume). (See Block 4.)

Correlate 3.3 Used here to describe factors which tend to be associated with the phenomenon being examined—in this case field-independence. Thus an ecological correlate is a factor in the ecology or environment which is found to be frequently associated with field dependence or independence, and a social correlate is a feature of social organization which is similarly associated.

Correlation Activity 2, Discussion The degree of relationship between two variables. This can be expressed statistically on a scale varying between +1.0 and −1.0. A positive correlation indicates that the variables vary with each other: high scores on one variable tend to be associated with high scores on the other, and low ones with low. Zero correlation means that there is no relationship, while a negative correlation means that high scores on one variable tend to be associated with low scores on the other (see Methodology Handbook).

Cultural bias   1.9   See 'ethnocentric'.

Cultural variables   1.6   Any dimension along which cultures may differ. Social structure, socialization practices, method of subsistence, art style and religion are a few of the many examples of cultural variables.

Deviation Quotient   6.10   A technique used by P. E. Vernon for making comparisons between scores on various tests administered to different cultural groups. Each test was standardized on a sample of one hundred British middle-class school boys to give a deviation quotient with a mean of one hundred and a standard deviation of fifteen, comparable to a conventional IQ. The deviation quotients of individuals or groups could then be compared with each other to see how they varied from the norms provided by the British sample.

Didactic learning   8.17   Learning through orders and instructions given by others. *Self-regulated learning* is, as the name implies, to do with learning about things for oneself, discovering general principles and rules, for example, through one's own efforts, and at one's own pace.

Ecology   1.5   The total environment i.e. the systematic interaction of all the plants, animals and people in a specific area with each other and with their physical surroundings.

Educational Priority Areas   7.9   In certain areas of special need, schools receive *positive discrimination* in the form of extra money for teachers, building programmes for schools and (from the Urban Aid Programme) extra nursery places.

Ego-centric sequences   8.28   Verbal sequences which are more often found when an elaborated code (see 'sociolinguistic codes') is being used. The sequence relates to the speakers *own* views i.e. the 'I' is emphasized over the 'we' of the group. *Socio-centric sequences* are the opposite of this—the group view or feeling being emphasized over the personal. The assumption that the person being spoken to shares the same views means that 'we' includes both speaker and listener.

Embedded Figures Test   3.9   A test designed to measure the degree of *field-dependence/independence*. It consists of a set of simple figures (e.g. a triangle or a square) and a set of complex figures (consisting of a composite geometrical design which is coloured and patterned). Each complex figure has one of the simple figures incorporated in its design. The subject being tested is shown one of the simple figures for a short period of time (e.g. ten seconds) and is then asked to identify it in one of the complex figures. People vary significantly in their ability to do this (see Block 5, Figure 11).

Ethnocentric   1.7   A viewpoint or approach in which one's own group or culture is regarded as the central reference point or standard and other groups are evaluated and compared with it. Ethnocentrism can be a hindrance to the objective and constructive study of different groups, particularly if it is implicit or unconscious and therefore unintentional. Ethnocentrism can also be described as cultural bias.

Ethnolinguistics   4.2   The study and comparison of different languages.

Field-dependence/independence   2.20   Described by H. A. Witkin, this is a dimension measuring psychological differentiation (see below) in the area of perception. Field-dependent people are less able to separate parts of the perceptual field from the whole than field-independent people (see Block 5, Section 3).

Foreshortening   2.10   Perspective applied to a single object. An arm pointing directly at the spectator so that little more than the hand can be seen is said to be strongly foreshortened.

Functional equivalent   1.9   Anything which serves the same or similar functions as something else but is different in structure or form. Social structures as well as actual objects can be functional equivalents. For example, several different types of family structure may all serve similar functions, such as socialization and care of the children providing a simple basis round which to run the economic organization of the household, etc.

g factor   6.13   This means general ability. It is described by Spearman as being the common factor in performance underlying the scores on tests which measure different abilities. He described it in terms of the positive correlation which normally exists between performance on two tests, e.g. a test measuring spatial ability and a test measuring verbal ability. He explained the difference in performance on the two tests by *s* factors, which are the skills specific to the particular tests. (See also 'group factor analysis' below, and Block 6, Part 1.)

Gene pool   6.5   The total genetic information possessed by the reproductive members of a population of sexually reproducing organisms.

Genetic encoding   2.1   This refers to the combination of genes which predetermine the hereditary components of an individual. This combination is the information which causes each cell to produce certain substances in particular quantities and combinations.

Genetic potential   6.5   The limitations carried in the genetic make-up of an individual. Thus the genetic make-up will limit the maximum height to which a person will grow, and the physical strength which he can attain. Such characteristics which vary in quantity, (e.g. height, strength and intelligence) are also affected by environmental influences. For example, bad diet or illness in childhood can prevent the maximum height, as determined by the genetic potential, from being realized. The minimum environmental requirement needed for the potential to be realized is known as the threshold (see Block 4).

Geo-spatial linguistic distinctions   Activity 4, Discussion   The way in which particular language distinguishes between different shapes and spatial relationships. Languages vary in the precision and number of distinctions made, and also in the properties of an object or a spatial array which are regarded as critical in a description.

Goodenough Draw-a-Man Test   6.9   A test of intelligence and maturity in which the subject is asked to draw a man, and sometimes also a woman. The drawing is then scored for its overall accuracy and also for its detail, such as the presence or absence of certain features e.g. eyebrows, fingers, etc. The score is compared to the norms provided.

Group factor analysis   6.3   Used to describe statistical procedure showing that, together with a *g* factor underlying the performance on all mental tests, and one or more *s* factors (factors relating to task specific skills) underlying the performance on a particular test, there is also correlation between particular groups of tests. Thus a hierarchical view of intelligence can be developed (see Block 6, Part 1).

Heredity-environment debate   6.1   See 'nature–nurture question'.

Hypothesis   2.7   Ideas put forward to explain a phenomenon. Most scientific experiments aim to prove or disprove a hypothesis.

Imaging skills   5.16   Used here to describe the ability to form images in thinking or writing. The images would normally be formed from previous experiences related to the subject of the thought. Thus, if a person wishes to re-arrange the furniture in his sitting room, he might form images of the room with the room and furniture in different positions. His past experience, i.e. his familiarity with the appearance of the room and furniture, is brought to bear on his present problem, i.e. what the room will look like with the furniture moved around.

Intelligence A, B and C   6.3   These are three suggested levels of intelligence. *Intelligence A* is the potential intelligence of an individual as determined by his genetic make-up (the genotype). *Intelligence B* is the product of the interaction between the individual and his environment (the phenotype). Thus it is a person's intelligence, as it is shown by his behaviour, incorporating all the concepts and descriptions which are commonly attributed to intelligence. *Intelligence C* is the expression of a person's intelligence as measured on a standardized intelligence test. The scores obtained may be regarded as a measure of Intelligence B; but the accuracy of the measure will depend on the validity and comprehensiveness of the tests used.

IQ (Intelligence Quotient)   6.1   During childhood this is an index of the rate of development of intelligence. It is found by determining the relationship of a child's mental age to his chronological age by means of his score on standardized tests. Among adults and children the IQ is also an index of the relative intelligence of an individual, as measured by his score on a standardized test compared to that of the general population. Its mean is 100 and its standard deviation is approximately sixteen.

Kohs Blocks design test   2.23   A test utilizing a set of one-inch coloured cubes whose sides are painted red, blue, yellow, white, yellow-and-blue, and red-and-white. Coloured designs are presented to the subject on test cards which he must reproduce using the blocks.

Lexical level   4.11   See 'lexicon'.

Lexicon   4.5   The total stock of words in a language. Thus to look at something at the lexical level is to look at it from the point of view of the stock of words available in the language.

Limiting factor   2.20   A factor which is critical to the development of a particular trait, feature or activity. For example, the number of frost-free days may be the limiting factor affecting the areas where citrus fruits may be grown, or the educational level of an individual may be a limiting factor affecting the degree to which he is able to interpret a 2–D representation of a 3–D scene.

Mixed class   8.14   Cook-Gumperz had a special index of social class constructed for her research into modes of control, which combined an occupational *and* an educational rating for both father and mother. The mixed class category contained parents who had either a job or educational experience which was discrepant, e.g. someone who had attended a grammar school until eighteen and gained some qualifications, but was working as a shop assistant.

Mode of control   8.13   Bernstein proposed three modes of verbal control: *the imperative mode* (e.g. you must do this); *the positional mode* (i.e. instructions given with reference to the status of the individual involved, e.g. you are too old for that); *the personal mode* (i.e. instructions given with reference to the personal qualities of the individuals involved, e.g. I know you don't want to give her a birthday present, but she'll be upset if you don't.).

Model   7.11   Used here to describe a number of co-ordinated working hypotheses brought together in order to systematize social phenomena and to give a simplified and schematized picture of reality. In the absence of general theories in social science, models (being systematizations of parts of social reality) are frequently developed, e.g. in understanding political parties, pressure groups, public opinions, urbanization, organization, etc.

Multiple-factor analysis   6.3   This type of factor analysis is very commonly used today and in practice can only be done with a computer. In multiple-factor analysis, the factors necessary to account for the correlation between tests are extracted. This is unlike Spearman's method or group-factor analysis, where the analyst places restrictions on the number and type of factors to be extracted from the data. (See Methodology Handbook for a fuller description.)

Myelination   3.11   The process whereby the fatty tissue (myelin) which surrounds nerve fibres is formed. Myelin insulates the electro-chemical activity in the nerves from other body tissue. The amount of myelination affects the speed at which signals can be carried along the nerve.

n Ach   8.23   As part of his general theory of personality, the psychologist H. A. Murray produced a list of forty four variables which he considered to be the most important in determining personality. Included in these variables he listed Needs and their related Presses. *Presses* are the external determinants of behaviour which come from the environment; *Needs* are the internal determinants of behaviour that come from within the individual. n Ach is Murray's shorthand for 'need achievement' which simply means the need for people to do well at things they attempt or in which they are involved (see Appendix A to Block 2).

Nature–nurture question   2.15   This is a fundamental question in the behavioural and social sciences, which often appears to be insoluble. Basically the question is how much and which parts of people's behaviour are inherited and inborn, and how much is due to learning and interaction with the environment? *The heredity-environment debate*, referred to in 6.1, is the same question, but it has come to be associated mainly with intelligence, i.e. is an individual's level of intelligence largely due to inherited factors or learning, or to interaction between the two? (see also Block 6, Part 1).

Norm   5.23   In its statistical sense this is a mean or modal value on some specified psychological dimension. The norms most commonly given for psychological tests state the average performance and the variability in performance of a representative sample to whom the test has been applied. The individual's score on a test can then be compared with these norms to see his performance in relation to the population at large (see also Methodology Handbook). Thus, in the context of Piagetian studies, norms are available on the ages at which people normally reach the various Piagetian stages and sub-stages. The stage attained by an individual is identified by his performance on various Piagetian tasks (e.g. conservation) or, at ages before the child can be formally tested, by observation.

Nurture groups   10.6   A project designed to provide a pre-school environment within the school for children who have not yet reached a level of emotional and cognitive maturity to enable them to cope in the normal school setting. Emphasis is placed on providing a secure, warm and relaxed environment for the children. The day is broken up with various routines which help the children to develop their self-control (see Television Programme 13, *Nurture Groups*).

Participant observation   7.17   Used here to contrast the social scientific observer who takes part in the way of life he is studying with one who watches but remains aloof.

Peers   9.2   People who are equal in status e.g. class mates, children of about the same age.

Perceptual inference habits   2.3   The way in which an individual normally interprets a visual image. Thus westerners commonly interpret a picture in which one object partly obscures another to mean that the complete object is in front of, and is therefore concealing, the rest of the other object—not that only part of one of the objects is present. Perceptual inference habits vary among people from different cultures and are influenced by many variables such as surrounding ecology, type of education, etc.

Perspective   2.3   A method of representing three dimensional objects on a flat surface, i.e. in two dimensions, so that they give the same impression of relative positions, size, etc. as the actual objects do when viewed from a particular point. Many art styles do not use this method of representing three dimensional objects, but concentrate on other aspects of the objects portrayed (e.g. split perspective, in which an object is represented as it would appear if it had been split down the middle and laid flat; twisted perspective, in which some parts of the object are portrayed in 'true' perspective and others are not, as in some ancient Egyptian work).

Piagetian stages   5.2   Piaget, through his detailed and rigorous observation of individual children over a long period of time, drew several important conclusions about the course of child development. His theory proposes that individuals go through four global stages during development. These appear in the following order:

Sensory-motor stage. This stage lasts from birth to the development of language—normally about eighteen months to two years. It is mainly concerned with developing and elaborating schemas which co-ordinate the infant's sensory perceptions with his actions.

Pre-operational stage. The second developmental stage, lasting from between the ages of about two and seven. This stage is mainly characterized by the development of language and the consolidation and integration of the child's syncretic reasoning processes where the operations system is still rather disorganized. The pre-operational stage culminates in the beginnings of the concrete operational stage where different operations become co-ordinated and integrated, though only in relation to actual situations.

Concrete operations. This stage occurs between the ages of seven and twelve. In the concrete operational stage the child has a well integrated system of operations, but can only apply these to actual situations, not hypothetical ones.

Formal operations. The final stage normally begins at about the age of twelve and will proceed to develop for about three years, though it may not be fully attained by everyone. This stage involves the ability to reason abstractly about a hypothetical problem using the organized operations system developed in the concrete operations stage. An 'operation', in Piagetian terms, is any skill or ability (schema) which has an organized and integrated structure behind it. Thus it is a schema with an underlying organization which can be used in any situation requiring this particular skill, e.g. classification. Various operations are linked together to form a coherent intellectual framework on which an individual can base his actions. An operation can also be defined as an internally represented action (see Block 4).

Plowden Report   7.9   More properly, *Children and Their Primary Schools,* 1967, a report of the Central Advisory Council for Education (England), two volumes, HMSO. A committee was set up in 1963, under the chairmanship of Lady Plowden, in order 'to consider primary education in all its aspects and the transition to secondary education'. It commissioned extensive research, and made many recommendations, some of which have been implemented. Its researchers suggested that parental *attitudes* have more influence on children's educational attainment than either their economic circumstances or the characteristics of their children's schools (see also the booklet, *Social Class and Educational Achievement*). Their recommendations included: channelling extra resources towards defined areas of the country (Educational Priority Areas), with research into the results; expanding nursery education; opening schools for community use; restricting the stages of primary (and secondary) education; ending corporal punishment in primary schools; ending streaming in junior schools; acceptance of 'child-centred' teaching methods.

Polygamy   3.7   Strictly the situation of a husband having more than one wife, *or* a wife having more than one husband, at any one time. The latter is fairly uncommon and polygamy, except in specialized anthropological literature, can be taken to mean more than one wife.

Positive discrimination   7.9   A decision to give selected groups, individuals, institutions or areas preferential treatment in order to raise their standards or status nearer to those of more advantaged groups. In educational terms, positive discrimination means that certain schools receive extra funds, teachers, equipment, etc.

Projective materials   1.5   Test materials consisting of ambiguous stimuli. The subject, in responding to these stimuli is supposed to project his own feelings, needs, attitudes, motives, etc. into his response. Stimuli used in such tests include ink-blots, pictures, incomplete sentences, story themes and single words (see also Block 2, Section 3).

Proprioceptive sense   3.13   See 'sense modalities'.

Psychological differentiation   3.1   Used by Witkin to summarize diverse expressions (in perception, thinking, body concept, sense of identity, etc.) of an underlying process of individual development towards a greater psychological complexity.

Rank-order correlation   3.10 Table 4   This is the correlation between two variables of which only the ranks are important. Thus, the correlation between the class-position of children in various subjects could only be calculated using a rank-order correlation coefficient, whereas correlations between examination scores could be calculated using the product-moment correlation coefficient (see Methodology Handbook).

Raven's Matrices   3.15   A non-verbal intelligence test in which the subject has to select, from a number of alternatives, the item which best completes a pattern (see Block 5, Figure 13).

Retina   2.1   A layer of light-sensitive nerve cells (rods and cones) covering the inner surface of the eye ball (see Block 4).

Rod and Frame Test   3.14   A test designed to measure field-dependence/independence. The subject sits in a darkened room and can see only a luminous square frame containing a straight rod. Both frame and rod can be rotated on a central pivot. The experimenter tilts the frame and asks the subject to align the rod with the vertical. Some subjects align the rod more with the sides of the frame, while others align it nearer to the true vertical. The chair in which the subject sits may also be tilted (see Block 5, Figure 10).

Role separation   Activity 4, Discussion   This is the same as role differentiation and is the degree to which the social roles referred to are separated, i.e. the extent of overlap. Thus the role of wife and mother overlaps to quite a large extent, whereas the roles of mother and club secretary do not.

Rorschach Inkblots Test   2.1   A projective test which consists of ten cards with symmetrical ink-blots on them. The subject is presented with the cards in a prescribed sequence and asked to say what the blots could be. Responses are interpreted as revealing various aspects of an individual's psychological make-up.

Sample   2.13   A group which is selected from a larger group (the 'parent population'), with the aim of inferring information about this population as a whole. Obviously the sample must be representative (i.e. similar in most respects to the larger population) if the data obtained is to be indicative of the performance of individuals in the larger population.

Schema   5.15   An element of organization, i.e. a characteristic way of responding to the environment. Thus a young infant will have a schema applicable to suckable objects, and he will treat any such object coming near his mouth accordingly. Schemas, being an already formed organization, provide the infant with a systematic and structured response to his environment. More sophisticated and differentiated schemas will develop as the child experiences increasingly varied environments, and as his cognitive powers develop and change. Schemas also exist to cope with situations which do not involve actual physical actions, e.g. characteristic ways of thinking about things, such as classification (see Block 4).

Self-regulated learning   8.17   See 'didactic learning'.

Sense modalities   3.3   Hearing, sight, taste, smell and touch (including here balance and awareness of bodily position with reference to the environment, and the position of parts of the body to others while the body is moving or stationary). This broad definition of touch is also known as the *proprioceptive sense* (see 3.13).

Social role 8.17   Denotes the type of social behaviour normally exhibited by particular categories of people e.g. the role of teacher or pupil. An individual normally has to play several roles, e.g. the role of pupil and son. Each role has an accompanying status and a person occupying a particular status has certain rights and duties towards others which he must take into account while acting in that role.

Social sanctions 3.7   Constraints or punishments which society can bring to bear on those who transgress social norms, e.g. 'sending to Coventry', or being ostracized from an 'in group'. These sanctions are more subtle, and often more implicit and less well defined, than legal ones exercised in a formal and structured way by authorized individuals.

Socialization 1.4   The process by which an individual learns the social processes and values of a particular society so that he can, to a greater or lesser degree, be accepted by and successfully interact with members of that society.

Socio-centric sequences 8.28   See 'ego-centric sequences'.

Sociolinguistic codes 8.26   Proposed by Bernstein, these (1) indicate the form of the social relationship in which the speech occurs: in the case of an *elaborated* code, the speakers will tend to be aware of individual differences, and have less formalized roles; in the case of a *restricted* code, speakers will have communalized roles and be less aware of individual differences; (2) regulate the nature of speech encounters: with an *elaborated* code, meanings are made explicit, accessible to the listener; with a *restricted* code, shared meanings need less verbalization, remain implicit, and are understood by the speakers; (3) create for the speaker a frame of reference. The *elaborated* code has a universalistic order of meaning in that principles (why things are done) and operations (how things are done) are made explicit. It is not tied to its context, and makes the speaker capable of detachment and therefore reflexiveness. A *restricted* code's order of meaning is 'particularistic': principles tend not to be verbalized, but remain implicit; meanings are context-bound, i.e. closely dependent on the speaker's situation, and tend to occur within close relationships and a local social group who share his attitudes, etc.

Standardized test 6.6   A test which has been tried on a representative sample of the population in order to provide adequate norms, and data on its reliability and validity. The results can safely be generalized to the population from which the sample is drawn, but not to any other population. A standardized test has set procedures for administration and scoring so that different results cannot normally be attributed to differences in these procedures. (See Section 3 of the Methodology Handbook.)

Sub-cultures 1.4   These are cultures which exist within the framework of a larger culture. In complex and varied societies, e.g. Britain, several sub-cultures, such as black immigrant and working class, can be identified. Members of a sub-culture, although adhering to a greater or lesser extent to the values and social norms of the wider culture, also have their own values and norms, and they may differ in social structure and patterns from the main culture of which they form a part. Usually when there are several different sub-cultures one of these becomes dominant, and its particular social patterns and values become the standard ones for the whole culture. (See Activity 8 for a discussion of class and sub-culture.)

Subsistence economies 3.2   Economies which only produce, by farming or hunting and gathering, the amount of food which is needed for survival, i.e. no surplus of food is generally available for trade.

Tribal norms 3.7   These are social norms as opposed to the statistical norms described under 'norm' in this glossary. Social norms are any attitudes, values, opinions etc. which are shared by members of a social group, and to which people are usually expected to conform.

Urban Aid Programme 7.9   This programme, introduced in 1968, was sponsored by five central government departments in an attempt to encourage the kind of schemes for urban areas which do not usually fall within local authority provision. Local authorities may submit projects for consideration, and those successful qualify for a 75 per cent grant, the remaining 25 per cent being found by the local authority. Voluntary agencies may also apply, but only through their local authority. The programme has been organized in a series of phases in which emphasis was at first put on building (e.g. nursery schools). Later phases have been more flexible, providing funds for services such as telephone advice, minibuses and mobile housemothers.

Value judgement   7.2   A subjective judgement based on the value an individual places on the objects which he is considering.

Values   1.11   Attitudes or opinions held by an individual which he feels to be correct or important. Where such values are held by the majority of individuals within a society, or by the individuals who exercise power and control over the other individuals in a society, they can be described as social norms.

Variable   2.13   An entity which may vary in a classifiable or measurable form. In a well constructed experiment, those variables not being specifically studied are as far as possible carefully controlled.

References

Titles marked with an asterisk are those recommended for further reading.

ANASTASI, A. (1968) *Psychological Testing* (3rd edn), London: MacMillan.

*BARNES, D., BRITTON, J., ROSEN, H. and the L.A.T.E. (1971) *Language, the learner and the school*, Harmondsworth, Penguin, revised edition.

BARRY, H., CHILD, I. L. and BACON, M. K. (1959) 'Relation of Child Training to Subsistence Economy', *American Anthropologist*, 61, pp. 51–63.

BEREITER, C. and ENGELMANN, S. (1966) *Teaching Disadvantaged Children in the Preschool*, New Jersey, Prentice-Hall.

BERNADONI, L. C. (1964) 'A culture fair intelligence test for the Ugh, No and Oo-La-La cultures', *Personnel and Guidance Journal*, 1964, 42 pp. 554–7.

BERNSTEIN, B. (1971) *Class, Codes and Control, Vol. I*, London, Routledge and Kegan Paul.

BERNSTEIN, B. (ed.) (1973) *Class, Codes and Control, Vol. 2*, London, Routledge and Kegan Paul.

BERRY, J. W. (1966) 'Temne and Eskimo perceptual skills', *International Journal of Psychology*, 1(3), pp. 207–229.

*BERRY, J. W. (1969) 'On cross-cultural comparability', *International Journal of Psychology*, 4(2), pp. 119–128.

BERRY, J. W. (1971) 'Müller–Lyer Susceptibility: Culture, Ecology or Race?', *International Journal of Psychology*, 6(3), pp. 193–197.

BERRY, J. W. (1971) 'Ecological and cultural factors in spatial perceptual development', *Canadian Journal of Behavioural Science*, 1971, 3, pp. 324–36.

BERRY, J. W. (in press) 'An Ecological Approach to Cross Cultural Psychology', *Netherlands Journal of Psychology*.

BONTÉ, M. (1962) 'The Reaction of two African Societies to the Müller–Lyer illusion', *Journal of Social Psychology*, 58, pp. 265–268.

BOVET, M. C. (1973) 'Cognitive processes among illiterate children and adults', in Berry, J. W. and Dasen, P. R. (eds.) (1974) *Culture and Cognition: Readings in Cross-cultural Psychology*, London, Methuen.

BOXALL, M. (1976) 'The Nurture Group in the Primary School', ILEA (internal report).

BROWN, R. W. and LENNEBERG, E. H. (1958) 'Studies in Linguistic Relativity' in Maccoby, E. E. *et al.* (eds.) *Readings in Social Psychology*, (3rd edn), London, Methuen.

BRUNER, J. S. *et al.* (eds.) (1966) *Studies in Cognitive Growth*, New York, John Wiley.

*BRUNER, J. S. (1974) *The Relevance of Education*, Harmondsworth, Penguin.

BULLOCK COMMITTEE (1975) *A Language for Life*, Report of the Committee of Inquiry (Chairman: Sir Alan Bullock), Department of Education and Science, HMSO.

BURT, C. (1937) *The Backward Child*, London, University of London Press.

BYNNER, J. M. (1972) *Parents' Attitudes to Education*, Office of Population Censuses and Surveys: Social Survey Division, London, HMSO.

CAZDEN, C. B. (1970) 'The neglected situation in child language research and education', in Williams, F. (ed) *Language and Poverty*, Chicago, Markham, pp. 81–101.

CARROLL, J. B. and CASAGRANDE, J. B. (1958) 'The function of language classifications in behaviour', in Maccoby, E. E. *et al.* (eds.) *Readings in Social Psychology*, (3rd edn), London, Methuen.

COLE, M. and BRUNER, J. S. (1971) 'Cultural differences and inferences about psychological processes', *American Psychologist*, 1971, 26, pp. 867–76.

COLEMAN, J. (1972) *How do the young become adults?*, Report No. 130, Centre for Social Organization of Schools, The John Hopkins University. (Reprinted in Raynor, J. and Harden, J. (eds.) Cities, Communities and the Young: Readings in Urban Education, Volume I, London, Routledge and Kegan Paul/The Open University Press.)

COOK-GUMPERZ, J. (1973) *Social Control and Socialization: A Study of Class Differences in the Language of Maternal Control*, London, Routledge and Kegan Paul.

DASEN, P. R. (1972) 'Cross-cultural Piagetian research; a summary', *Journal of Cross-cultural Psychology*, 3(1), pp. 23–39.

DASEN, P. R. (1974) 'The influence of ecology, culture and European contact on cognitive development in Australian Aborigines', in Berry, J. W. and Dasen, P. R. (eds.) (1974) *Culture and Cognition: Readings in Cross-cultural Psychology*, London, Methuen.

DAVIE, R., BUTLER, N. and GOLDSTEIN, H. (1972) *From Birth to Seven: A Report of the National Child Development Study*, London, Longman (in association with The National Children's Bureau).

DAWSON, J. L. M. (1967) 'Cultural and Physiological influences upon spatial–perceptual processes in West Africa—parts 1 and 2', *International Journal of Psychology*, 2, pp. 115–128 and 171–185.

DENNIS, W. (1966) 'Goodenough scores, art experience and modernization', *Journal of Social Psychology*, 68, pp. 211–228.

DENNIS, W. (1966) *Group Values through Children's Drawings*, New York, John Wiley.

DEREGOWSKI, J. B. (1967) 'The horizontal–vertical illusion and the ecological hypothesis', *International Journal of Psychology*, Vol. 2, No. 4, pp. 269–273.

DEREGOWSKI, J. B. (1972) 'Pictorial perception and culture', *Scientific American*, pp. 82–88.

EZARD, J. (1974) 'Way off the mark?', *The Guardian*, 16.7.74.

*FRIEDMAN, N. L. (1967) 'Cultural deprivation: a commentary in the sociology of knowledge', *Journal of Educational Thought*, 1(2) pp. 88–99.

*GAY, J. and COLE, M. (1967) *The New Mathematics and an Old Culture*, New York, Holt, Rinehart and Winston.

GLADWIN, T., (1964) 'Culture and logical process', in Berry, J. W. and Dasen, P. R. (eds). (1974) *Culture and Cognition: Readings in Cross-cultural Psychology*, London, Methuen.

GLADWIN, T. (1970) *East is a Big Bird*, Cambridge, Mass., Harvard University Press.

*GLICK, J. (1969) 'Culture and Cognition: some theoretical and methodological concerns', in Spindler, G. D. (ed.) (1974) *Education and Cultural Process*, New York, Holt, Rinehart and Winston.

GOODACRE, E. J. (1968) *Teachers and their pupils' home background*, Slough, NFER.

GOODNOW, J. and BETHON, G. (1966) 'Piaget's Tasks: The effects of schooling and intelligence', *Child Development*, 37, pp. 573–582.

GOODNOW, J. J. (1970) 'Cultural variations in cognitive skills', *Cognitive Studies*, 1970, 1, pp. 242–57.

GREENFIELD, P. MARKS, (1966) 'On culture and conservation' in Bruner, J. S., Olver, R. R. and Greenfield, P.M. (eds.) *Studies in Cognitive Growth* (Ch. 11), New York, Wiley, pp. 225–56.

GREGOR, A. J. and McPHERSON, D. A. (1965) 'A study of susceptibility to geometric illusion among cultural subgroups of Australian Aborigines', *Psychologica Africana*, 11, pp. 1–13.

GREGORY, R. L. (1966) *Eye and Brain: the Psychology of Seeing*, London, Weidenfeld and Nicolson.

GUTMAN, D. (1969) 'Psychological naturalism in cross-cultural studies', Willems, E. P. and Raush, H. L. (eds.) *Naturalistic Viewpoints in Psychological Research*, New York, Holt, Rinehart and Winston.

HARGREAVES, D. H., HESTER, S. K. and MELLOR, F. J. (1975) *Deviance in Classrooms*, London, Routledge and Kegan Paul.

*HEAD, D. (ed.) (1974) *Free Way to Learning*, Harmondsworth, Penguin Education Special.

HESS, R. D. and SHIPMAN, V. C. (1965) 'Early experience and the socialization of cognitive modes in children', *Child Development*, 36(3), pp. 869–86.

HOLT, J. (1965) *How Children Fail*, London, Pitman (reissued Penguin, 1969).

*HORTON, R. (1967) 'African Traditional Thought and Western Science' in Wilson, B. R. (ed.) (1970) *Rationality*, Blackwell. Also reprinted in Young, M. F. D. (ed.) *Knowledge and Control: New Directions for the Sociology of Education* (1971) Collier-MacMillan.

HOUSTON, S. H. (1971) 'A re-examination of some assumptions about the language of the disadvantaged child', Chess, S. and Thomas, A. (eds.) *Annual Progress in Child Psychiatry and Child Development*, Butterworth.

HUDSON, W. (1960) 'Pictorial depth perception in sub-cultural groups in Africa', *Journal of Social Psychology*, 52, pp. 183–208.

HUDSON, W. (1967) 'The study of the problem of pictorial perception among unacculturated groups', *International Journal of Psychology*, Vol. 2, pp. 90–107.

IRVINE, S. H. (1969) 'Contributions of ability and attainment testing in Africa to a general theory of intellect', *Journal of Biosocial Science*, Supplement No. 1, pp. 91–102. Included in Berry, J. W. and Dasen, P. R. (eds.) (1974) *Culture and Cognition: Readings in Cross-Cultural Psychology*, London, Methuen.

JACKSON, B. and MARSDEN, D. (1962) *Education and the Working Class*, London, Routledge and Kegan Paul.

JAHODA, G. (1966) 'Geometric illusions and environment; a study in Ghana', *British Journal of Psychology*, Vol. 57, pp. 193–9.

JAHODA, G. (1971) 'Retinal pigmentation, illusion susceptibility and space perception', *International Journal of Psychology*, 6(3), pp. 199–208.

JAHODA, G. and McGURK, H. (1974) 'Development of pictorial depth perception: cross-cultural replications', *Child Development*, 45, pp. 1042–1047.

JENCKS, C. et al. (1973) *Inequality*, London, Allen Lane.

JONCICH, G. (1964) 'A culture-bound concept of creativity: a social historian's critique, centering on a recent American research report', *Educational Theory*, 14(3), 133–143.

*KEDDIE, N. (ed.) (1973) *Tinker Tailor . . . The Myth of Cultural Deprivation*, Harmondsworth, Penguin.

*KOHL, H. R. (1970) *The Open Classroom*, London, Methuen.

LABOV, W. (1970) 'The Logic of non-standard English' in Williams, F. (ed.) *Language and Poverty*, Chicago, Markham.

LACEY, C. (1966) 'Some sociological concomitants of academic streaming in a grammar school', *British Journal of Sociology*, 14, 245–62.

LANTZ, D. and STEFFLRE, V. (1964) 'Language and cognition revisited', *Journal of Abnormal and Social Psychology*, 69(5), pp. 472–481.

LEACOCK, E. B. (ed.) (1971) *The Culture of Poverty: a Critique*, New York, Simon and Schuster.

*LLOYD, B. B. (1972) *Perception and Cognition: a Cross-cultural Perspective*, Harmondsworth, Penguin.

LUNN, J. C. B. (1972) 'The influence of sex, achievement level, and social class on Junior School children's attitudes', *British Journal of Educational Psychology*, 41(1), pp. 70–4.

MCFIE, J. (1961) 'Effects of education on African performance on a group of intellectual tests', *British Journal of Educational Psychology*, (31), pp. 232–240.

MIDWINTER, E. (1972) *Social Environment and the Urban School*, London, Ward Lock Educational.

MORTON-WILLIAMS, R. and FINCH, S. (1968) *Young School Leavers: Schools Council Enquiry 1*, London, HMSO.

MORTON-WILLIAMS, R. and FINCH, S. (1968) *Young School Leavers: Schools Council Enquiry 1*, London, HMSO.

MUSGROVE, F. (1966) *The Family, Education and Society*, London, Routledge and Kegan Paul.

NASH, R. (1973) *Classrooms Observed*, London, Routledge and Kegan Paul.

NEWSON, J. and NEWSON, E. (1965) *Patterns of Infant Care in an Urban Community*, Harmondsworth, Penguin.

NEWSON, J. and NEWSON, E. (1970) *Four Years Old in an Urban Community*, Harmondsworth, Penguin.

NEWTON, B. (1975) 'A language for life—or school?' *Times Educational Supplement*, 13.6.75, p. 17.

PLOWDEN COMMITTEE (1967) *Children and their Primary Schools*, Report of the Central Advisory Council for Education (Chairman: Lady Plowden), Department of Education and Science, London, HMSO.

*POSTMAN, N. (1970) 'Illiteracy in America: Position Papers—The Politics of Reading', *Harvard Educational Review*, 40(2), pp. 244–52.

PRICE-WILLIAMS, D. R. (1961) 'A study concerning concepts of conservation of quantities among primitive children', *Acta Psychologica*, 18, pp. 297–305.

ROBBINS COMMITTEE (1963–4) *Higher Education*, Report of the Committee (Chairman: Lord Robbins) appointed by the Prime Minister, Cmnd. 2154, Department of Education and Science, London, HMSO.

ROSENTHAL, R. and JACOBSON, L. (1968) *Pygmalion in the Classroom*, New York, Holt, Rinehart and Winston.

RUTTER, M., YULE, W. and BERGER, M. (1974) 'The Children of West Indian Migrants', *New Society* (14.3.74), pp. 630–633.

SEARLE, C. (1972) *The Forsaken Lover: White Words and Black People*, Harmondsworth, Penguin.

SEGALL, M. W., CAMPBELL, D. T. and HERSKOVITS, M. S. (1966) *The Influence of Culture on Visual Perception*, Indianapolis, Bobbs-Merrill Co. Inc.

SHEPARD, S. (1965) *How Should We Educate the Deprived Child?*, Washington D.C. Council for Basic Education.

SMEDSLUND, J. (1961) 'The acquisition of conservation of substance and weight in children', *The Scandinavian Journal of Psychology*, 2, pp. 71–84.

SWIFT, D. F. (1966) 'Social class and achievement motivation', in *Educational Research*, 8, pp. 83–95.

SWIFT, D. F. (1968) 'Social class and educational adaptation', in Butcher, H. J. (ed.) *Educational Research in Britain*, 1, London, University of London Press, pp. 282–96.

SWIFT, D. F. (1973) 'Sociology and educational research', in Taylor, W. (ed.) *Research Perspectives in Education*, London, Routledge and Kegan Paul.

*TIZARD, B. (1975) *Early Childhood Education: A review and discussion of research in Britain*, Slough: NFER (2nd edn).

TURNBULL, C. M. (1961) *The Forest People: A Study of the Pygmies of the Congo*, New York, Simon and Schuster.

VERNON, P. E. (1969) *Intelligence and Cultural Environment*, London, Methuen.

WAX, M. L. and WAX, R. H. (1971) 'Cultural deprivation as an educational ideology', in Leacock, E. B. (ed.) *The Culture of Poverty: A Critique*, New York, Simon and Schuster.

WEDGE, P. and PROSSER, H. (1973) *Born to Fail?*, London, Arrow Books in association with The National Children's Bureau.

WHITEHEAD, J. M. (ed.) (1975) *Personality and Learning 1*, London, Hodder and Stoughton/The Open University Press (Course Reader).

WHORF, B. L. (1940) 'Science and linguistics', *Technology Review*, 42, pp. 229–231, 247–8.

WISEMAN, S. (1968) 'Educational deprivation and disadvantage', in Butcher, H. J. (ed.) *Educational Research in Britain, Vol. 1*, London, University of London Press Ltd. (See also Plowden Report Vol. 2, Appendix 9).

WITKIN, H. A. and ASCH, S. E. (1948) 'Studies in space orientation, IV: Further experiments on perception of the upright with displaced visual fields', *Journal of Experimental Psychology, Vol. 38*, pp. 762–82.

WITKIN, H. A. (1967) 'Cognitive styles across cultures', Berry, J. W. and Dasen, P. R. (eds.) (1974) *Culture and Cognition: Readings in Cross-cultural Psychology*, London, Methuen.

WOBER, M. (1966) 'Sensotypes', *Journal of Social Psychology*, 70, pp. 181–9.

WOBER, M. (1967) 'Adapting Witkin's field independence theory to accommodate new information from Africa', *British Journal of Psychology*, 58, pp. 29–38.

WOBER, M. (1974) 'Towards an understanding of the Kiganda concept of intelligence', Berry, J. W. and Dasen, P. R. (eds.) *Culture and Cognition: Readings in Cross-cultural Psychology*, London, Methuen.

WOLFSON, J. (ed.) (1976) *Personality and Learning 2*, London, Hodder and Stoughton/The Open University Press (Course Reader).

Acknowledgements

Grateful acknowledgement is made to the following sources for material used in this block:

Text

Extract from M. Boxall, *Principles and Practice of Nurture*, ILEA Schools Psychological Service, 1974; Extract from Jerome S. Bruner, *The Relevance of Education*, W. W. Norton and Co. Inc., copyright © 1971, 1973 Jerome S. Bruner; Extract from J. Glick, 'Culture and cognition: some theoretical and methodological concerns', in G. Spindler (ed.), *Educational and Cultural Process*, copyright Holt, Rinehart and Winston, 1974; Extract from Joyce Little, *Supplementary Service to Schools*, London Borough of Waltham Forest, 1975; Extract from B. Tizard, *Early Childhood Education*, NFER Publishing Co., 2nd ed., 1975; Extract from B. L. Whorf, 'Science and linguistics', *Technology Review*, MIT Press, 1940.

Figures

Figure 1 from M. W. Segall *et al.*, *The Influence of Culture on Visual Perception*, The Bobbs-Merrill Company Inc., 1966; *Figure 2* from W. Hudson, 'Pictorial depth perception in sub-cultural groups in Africa', *Journal of Social Psychology*, Vol. 52, 1960; *Figure 3* from Pierre R. Dasen, 'Cross-cultural Piagetian research: a summary', *Journal of Cross-cultural Psychology*, Vol. 3, No. 1, March 1972, Sage Publications Inc.; *Figure 4* from P. E. Vernon, *Intelligence and Cultural Environment*, Methuen, 1969; *Figure 5* from R. Davie *et al.*, *From Birth to Seven: A Report of the National Child Development Study*, Longman in association with The National Children's Bureau, 1972; *Figure 6* from P. Wedge and H. Prosser, *Born to Fail*, Arrow Books in association with the National Children's Bureau, 1973; *Figure 7* from R. Norton-Williams and S. Finch, *Young Schoolleavers: A Schools Council Enquiry I*, reproduced by permission of the Controller, HMSO.

Tables

Table 1 from W. Hudson, 'Pictorial depth perception in sub-cultural groups in Africa', *Journal of Social Psychology*, Vol. 52, 1960; *Tables 2, 3 and 4* from J. L. M. Dawson, 'Cultural and physiological influences upon spatial-perceptual processes in West Africa', *International Journal of Psychology*, Vol. 2, 1967, reproduced by permission of the International Union of Psychological Science and Dunod Editeur, Paris; *Table 5* adapted from M. Wober, 'Adapting Witkin's field independence theory to accommodate new information from Africa', *British Journal of Psychology*, Vol. 58, 1967; *Table 6* from M. Wober, 'Sensotypes', *Journal of Social Psychology*, Vol. 70. 1966; *Table 7* from P. E. Vernon, *Intelligence and Cultural Environment*, Methuen, 1969; *Table 8* from S. H. Irvine, 'Contributions of ability and attainment testing in Africa to a general theory of intellect', *Journal of Biosocial Science*, Blackwell Scientific, 1969; *Table 9* as Figure 6; *Table 10* adapted from J. and E. Newson, *Four Years Old in an Urban Community*, Allen and Unwin.

Illustrations

P. 10 top left and middle left (from a collection of the bills of mortality in London during the Plague year) Royal Statistical Society; *p. 10 top right* Imago Mortis from Hartmann Schedel, *Liber Chronicarum*, printed by Anton Koberger, Nuremberg, 1493, reprinted by permission of the Syndics of the University Library, Cambridge; *p. 10 middle right* Kenneth Lindley; *p. 10 bottom* from *Akenfield*, Angle Films; *p. 11* J. Allan Cash; *p. 15* Christopher Davies (*Report*, London); *pp. 50 and 51* Anne Bolt; *p. 65* Chris Schwarz; *p. 66* Charles Marriott and Chris Schwarz; *p. 95* United Artists Corporation Ltd.